The Great Takeover

How materialism, the media
and markets now dominate our lives

Carol Craig

ARGYLL✚PUBLISHING

© Carol Craig 2012

Argyll Publishing
Glendaruel
Argyll PA22 3AE

www.argyllpublishing.co.uk
www.centreforconfidence.co.uk
www.postcardsfromscotland.co.uk

The author has asserted her moral rights.

British Library Cataloguing-in Publication Data.

A catalogue record for this book is available from the British Library.

ISBN 978 1 908931 06 1

Printing
Martins the Printers, Berwick upon Tweed

Postcards from Scotland

Series editor: Carol Craig

Advisory group:
Fred Shedden, Chair, Centre for Confidence and Well-being;
Professor Phil Hanlon;
Jean Urquhart MSP

ACKNOWLEDGEMENTS

I would like to thank the following for their comments on the first draft of this book: Phil Hanlon, Fred Shedden, Alan Sinclair, Katherine Trebeck and Greg Lucas. I'd also like to thank Maggie Clark, Linda Kirkwood and Emily Cutts for their encouragement to write this book. Thanks are also due to Archie Dalrymple for helping me with the references and on-line material.

I also want to thank Zara Kitson. I met Zara at an event on materialism held by the Centre I run. I was extremely impressed by her instinctive understanding of the issues and her commitment to campaign for change. Zara agreed to be a collaborator in the book and her name appeared on the early publicity. However, Zara managed to secure a job and the pressure of work commitments, and the tight publishing deadline, meant that she did not have the time to contribute. Our early discussions did, nonetheless, help me think through some of the issues. She hopes to be involved in some of the follow-up materials and activities.

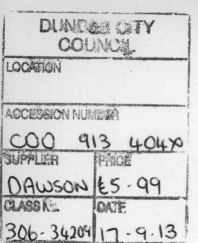

CONTENTS

INTRODUCTION

Do you ever feel that there is something rotten at the core of modern life? Are you concerned about the world your children, or grandchildren, are growing up in? If so, this book may help you understand what's gone wrong. It describes how materialist values, the media and business have come to *take over* our lives and how we are poorer for it both as individuals and as a society. The word *materialism* is used in this book to mean the pursuit of money and what it can buy, a focus on appearance and image and an emphasis on fame and power.

Over the past decade thinkers from all disciplines and backgrounds have written extensively on some of these issues but mainly approach it from a particular angle such as psychology, economics, the media or morality. My aim here is not to write an in-depth, comprehensive account of the problem. Instead I seek to help readers see the connections between developments which at face value seem unconnected and disparate. More importantly, by laying out some of the arguments and research in a small book, I hope to encourage people, who would be put off by a weighty volume, to engage with the topic.

I am the series editor for *Postcards from Scotland* which aims to present interesting ideas and perspectives on contemporary issues but in an accessible and inexpensive format. This is the second in the series. Some readers may be challenged and annoyed by the fact that, on the surface, this book is not very Scottish. Indeed there are many more references in the text to America and the UK than to Scotland. There are three main reasons for this. The first is that the rise of materialism and consumerism has been driven by developments in the American economy and culture and exported to the whole UK via shared media, business practices and converging politics. This then leads to the second point: the way in which Westminster government decisions and the mainstream British media have encouraged rampant materialist values to take root throughout the UK. Scotland has had its own devolved parliament since 1999 but the issues I'm addressing here, though of fundamental importance to Scotland, are not, by and large, the type of issues which the devolved Scottish government can control. Thirdly, while I cite Scottish data when I can, many of the research studies I quote come from UK samples.

Rising materialism is a growing international phenomenon – as countries Westernise and modernise the values inherent in materialism rise. Nonetheless there is some variation in their strength from country to country. Scandinavian countries support these values to a much lesser extent than Anglo-American states which have adopted 'turbo-capitalism'.

And what about Scotland? The remoter areas of rural Scotland are not only distant from commercial centres and pressures but also live more closely with nature, have stronger communities than urban areas and have managed to maintain some of their traditional cultures – all factors which are likely to help them maintain robust defences against the materialism of our age. But Scotland's central belt appears to be as materialistic as anywhere else in the UK. Glasgow was once world famous for what it produced and the skills of its workforce. Now the city is sold internationally as a centre of style and shopping even though the style is rarely designed or produced in the city. Even the debate on Scotland's future has been discussed and presented in essentially materialistic terms. Indeed one survey found that 65 per cent of Scots would vote for independence if it would make them £500 better off; 66 per cent would vote against if they would be £500 worse off. So Scotland's constitutional status could turn on such a small percentsge of average household income. As the economist John Kay writes: ' "Give me liberty or give me death," proclaimed Patrick Henry, arousing American colonists to rebellion with a cry reminiscent of the Declaration of Arbroath. "Give me liberty or give me £500" lacks the same resonance.'

Materialism is a major force in Scottish life and we need to ask ourselves if we want this to continue. Indeed as Scotland is a small country where it's feasible for discussions to take place in a variety of arenas, our conversation on this theme could have international relevance given that many countries also have to grapple with these issues – hence *Postcards from Scotland*.

This is a difficult topic to write about. Materialist values have been steadily rising for over thirty years and we're *all* caught up in them. I don't want to give the impression that I live a perfect life free of these values. This leads to another point which I would like the reader to bear in mind. When it comes to materialism in our everyday lives it is about *balance*. I'm not arguing for a hair-shirt existence. Of course, people are going to care about their appearance, their standard of living and how they are seen by others. The question is one of degree. Are these values part of people's lives or are they what's driving their lives? So when reading the following chapters please remember that what I'm arguing for is a healthier balance.

Also, this book has been challenging to write as it telescopes an enormous topic into a very short book. This means that I simply don't have the time to give nuanced messages and focus almost exclusively on what's wrong with materialism and its potentially negative effects on people. There's a rising tide of mental distress with more people succumbing to its ill effects and the book tries to show why materialism can undermine people's sense of themselves, their relationships and their mental health. Nonetheless the majority still manage to survive the onslaught of materialism and are remarkably resilient though they might still benefit if they took steps to protect themselves from its potentially deleterious effects.

The telescoping of the arguments also means that the book probably comes over as 'anti-business'. For reasons that will become evident in later chapters, our market dominated society is losing touch with morality and business is increasingly acting in ways which increase market share but at the expense of the wider society. Those running businesses have also become increasingly unfair in their treatment of employees. Nonetheless I accept that we need entrepreneurship and private business to create wealth and jobs and I cannot envisage a good society where the state runs everything. I'm particularly positive about family businesses which usually have a commitment and loyalty not just to staff but also to the local community.

A final point to bear in mind is that many of the problems I highlight in this book are mental and so increasingly invisible to a casual observer. Here's an example of what I mean. At the turn of the century inequality took the form of real physical poverty: poor children were hungry, dirty and unshod and lived in squalor while affluent children had all their material wants provided and lived in comfortable conditions. Today rich and poor children alike have shoes but are they the right shoes? So youngsters' shoes, and lots of other goods, are now important not because they have anything to do with real material need and well-being; their value is utterly symbolic. Shoes are no longer about keeping the feet warm, dry and uninjured – they are about self-esteem, how someone is judged and their place in society. Indeed because items such as shoes have such symbolic significance, mothers will even skimp on food and take on debt to buy their children the right symbols to avoid feeling excluded and stigmatised. So I freely admit that on the surface of society many things look fine but probe a bit deeper, and consider the data for mental health and other diseases of modern life, and a much more worrying picture emerges.

One of the great advantages of short books is that people are more likely to read them and, if enough do this in a small country like Scotland, then we can have a powerful discussion about whether we want to challenge these prevailing values and practices. To keep this book short I've put the references on-line. (A full set of references is contained in the Kindle edition). You can download a document with notes and references for the text so that you can follow up, or check sources, for all the quotes in this book.[1]

[1.] Please go to the Great Takeover section on www.postcardsfromscotland.co.uk.

CHAPTER ONE

Counting the costs

On a cold winter's evening in 2011 the Centre I run held an event with the catchy title 'Glasgow: Well-being, materialism and the values of consumer capitalism'. The 4th of December at 5 o'clock is not a great time for an event but was the only possible slot for our guest speaker in his fleeting visit to Scotland. Our publicity had also been minimal – one email to our database. Surprisingly 110 registered for the event but, since it was free and this often means no-shows, we skimped on the mince pies and were rather casual about the number of seats. So to our great surprise 125 – many more than anticipated – turned up and packed the room.

In the ensuing discussion it became evident that many had travelled long distances to attend. Of course, some came because they lived or worked in Glasgow and disapproved of how their city is actively marketed for shopping and style. But a surprising number had travelled from the north and east because the topic resonated: they were there because they wanted to hear and discuss what Professor Kasser's lecture on materialism meant for them and their families. One member of my Board commented later that he couldn't remember another event where men were unable to speak because women dominated the discussion.

I've also given lots of talks to a variety of different audiences on this subject and know that people are always interested and want to know more. Indeed a number of sound engineers as they've removed my microphone have often muttered – 'I couldn't agree more.' One even told me that if I stood for election he would vote for me.

So what's so special about the topic that it not only resonates with people, but motivates them as well?

Materialism and individual well-being

Tim Kasser is an American psychologist who has studied materialism for more than twenty years and he presents the core of research in his very accessible book *The High Price of Materialism* (2002). His research began in 1993 when he and a colleague started to examine college students' values via their 'Aspiration Index'. Much to their surprise they found that male and female students who thought 'financial success' of great importance had more anxiety and depression than those, for example, who valued 'community feeling' or 'self-actualisation' – a fancy term for personal development.

These researchers were intrigued: was this just a rogue result applying to students or was something more significant going on? They broadened their Index to include two other prominent values in consumer culture – image and fame – and now investigated older adults' views:

> The findings largely corroborated those reported
> with young adults. Adults who focused on money,
> image, and fame reported less self-actualisation and
> vitality, and more depression than those less

concerned with these values. What is more, they also reported significantly more experiences of physical symptoms. That is, people who believed it is important to strive for possessions, popularity and good looks also reported more headaches, backaches, sore muscles, and sore throats than individuals less focused on such goals.

Subsequently Kasser undertook numerous research projects using different methodologies and different groups but the findings were always the same. Other researchers report identical results. For example, one study of mental disorders in adolescents found that 'the priority put on being rich was related positively to almost every diagnosis assessed in this study, for the most part significantly so. . .'

This finding that materialistic values are associated with low well-being has been replicated in studies throughout the world, including the UK. A common conclusion is that the pursuit of money is associated with lowered life satisfaction – not the picture that advertising portrays.

So why do materialist values undermine well-being? Before answering it's necessary to point out that as we live in a material world some degree of materialism is not only natural but necessary. We need food and shelter to survive and a sense of security and comfort adds enormously to the quality of life. So it pays to place some value on material goods and in the modern world this means some awareness of the importance of money.

We can also see from archaeology that people, even cave-dwellers, have always devoted time and energy to their appearance. This is partly because appearance is linked to sexual attractiveness and thus to mating. What's more, the face, hair and body can all be used creatively to express individuality or a person's social role. So one way or another human beings are always going to consider, and care about, their appearance.

Equally, human beings are extremely social and so we're always going to pay attention to our status within the group and want to feel some degree of pride in our accomplishments. This means caring, to some extent, about how we are viewed by others.

So the problem with materialism is largely a matter of degree. Kasser argues that 'materialism is relative. Materialistic values become unhealthy when they are highly important in comparison with other values for which we might strive. The question is one of balance. . .' Kasser's rule of thumb is that materialism is detrimental to our well-being when it compromises the fulfillment of our fundamental psychological needs.

Before looking at what these needs are it's important to point out that wealth is not a good indicator of how materialistic a person is. Someone who is well-off could have inherited or won money, or they could be in a well-paid job which they love. In short, pursuit of money may not have been their goal. Compare this with another person with less money but who would 'sell their granny' to get on. Also, someone who has money, but who isn't driven by materialistic values, won't continually spend to impress others but will use their money to fulfill self-directed goals. Someone with a strong materialistic drive, however, will continually upgrade their possessions to impress others even if this means substantial debt.

Basic psychological needs

Kasser defines needs in terms of the framework set out by

Deci and Ryan in Self-Determination Theory (SDT). This argues from international, empirical research that human beings have basic psychological needs for relatedness, competence and autonomy. Let's look at what these mean and how materialism can undermine them.

Relatedness simply refers to the human need to feel a sense of belonging and connectedness with others. It's also about feeling appreciated and valued and participating in social groups. Materialist values can easily distract us from this basic need. Indeed Kasser argues from research that those with a materialistic orientation to life care less about warm, intimate relationships and take a more instrumental view of others. In other words, if people focus on making money and getting on they often sacrifice their intimate and family relationships and their involvement with community.

Autonomy does not mean independence from others. Rather it means having a sense of control. This might be as simple as being able to say 'no' or 'yes' for yourself and for your life not to be determined by others. Those with materialistic values, however, are overly concerned with outer appearances and image rather than something which is meaningful to themselves and which they have some control over. So, for example, materialistic people may pursue money and success to impress others but in the process compromise their own freedom and feelings of authenticity.

The need to feel competent is about experiencing ourselves as capable of controlling the environment and bringing about desired outcomes. In short, to feel effective. However, under the influence of materialist values people opt to do things, not because they are naturally interested or for the positive satisfaction of learning, but because they want financial success or accolades from others. So, for example, a young person may choose to study law for status and money rather than go to art school and pursue his or her passion.

Given all this it is easy to see why Kasser believes that one of the main problems with materialism is that it encourages us to pursue goals such as money, image, fame and popularity which are *extrinsic* to ourselves. In other words, we want these things in order to receive external recognition, reward or praise. The consequence of this is that we do things for the reward not for the satisfaction. Intrinsic goals, on the other hand, involve valuing something because it's inherently satisfying or meaningful, such as relationships with others, the community or personal growth. Holding extrinsic goals not only undermines intrinsic goals but affects many aspects of life thus making it less likely that we'll flourish and feel fulfilled or authentic.

Of course there are other less overtly 'psychological' explanations for why the pursuit of materialist values undermines well-being. For example, a sedentary and passive lifestyle filled with television and shopping reduces exercise, which is important for well-being and also takes us away from contact with nature and green spaces. Lots of studies have shown that the green world is fundamental to our physical and mental well-being.

Materialism also encourages us to believe that buying things makes us happy. There's little doubt that for most people, particularly women, shopping for non-routine goods is a pleasurable activity. Indeed making a purchase can even boost dopamine in the brain. However, the pleasure of shopping is short-lived. We may think that this new dress will boost our happiness but the new item is quickly integrated into our lives and forgotten. Even the purchase of large items such as a car or a kitchen does not have the power to transform our lives in the way we anticipate. Within a few weeks it's just our kitchen and we hardly notice it any more. Psychologists call this effect 'habituation'. They also use the term 'the hedonic treadmill' to convey the idea that a person's level of happiness is not affected long term by purchases or other types of pleasure. As Professor David Myers, an expert on happiness, said at one of my Centre's events: 'Happiness is less a matter of getting what we want than wanting what we have.'

Materialism's affect on other aspects of life

Kasser commenced his research on materialism over thirty years ago and now with the advent of a whole range of new media and the dominance of a virulent celebrity culture, his work seems prescient. Indeed the way extrinsic, materialist values have come to dominate – to literally take over our lives – is one of the great challenges of our times. Focusing on the growth of materialism can help us understand a range of apparently disparate trends such as our growing obsession with appearance (as witnessed by the huge surge in cosmetic surgery), the dominance of business values in all walks of life, brand snobbery, the predominance of reality television, the rise of magazines about celebrities' lives, and the increasing desire youngsters have to be famous just for the sake of it.

In the first book in this series, public health experts Phil Hanlon and Sandra Carlisle set out the growing problem of alcohol and drug use, particularly in Scotland (now 6th in the world for illegal drug use and 8th for alcohol consumption). They are convinced that these 'dis-eases' are in part manifestations of our materialistic and consumerist culture. A number of researchers, including Tim Kasser, have indeed found that people who score high on materialism are more likely to smoke, drink and take drugs.

For decades now research has shown that pursuing materialist values reduces well-being so we shouldn't be surprised that as these values have become more dominant in people's lives mental health problems have also risen. Indeed the World Health Organisation argues that the main health challenges of the future are mental not physical.

Mental health is the focus of Oliver James's book *Affluenza* (2007). James describes the predominance of materialist values as a 'virus' which is causing widespread sickness and distress. His diagnosis results from the interviews he conducted, mainly with rich people, in various countries and from a selection of objective data. His thesis is that the strain of virus generated by American style 'selfish capitalism' is particularly nasty and has had a profoundly negative effect not only on America but also on the UK and other English speaking countries which have embraced it. James presents evidence to support his claim that English speaking nations have rates of 'emotional distress' which 'are at least twice as high as those in mainland Western Europe'. He tells us: 'the more like America a society becomes, the higher its rate of emotional distress.'

Depression is the most common mental disorder and it's often accompanied by a crisis of meaning; a feeling that life is pointless. As one of the most common critiques of material-ism is that it empties life of all meaning, it's hardly surprising that as it has become more important in people's lives rates of depression have risen. Consumer societies like ours also depend on dissatisfaction. Indeed it's personal dissatisfaction which drives the great wheel of consumption. A few years ago I ran workshops in Glasgow, Bathgate and Inverness with a range of factory and office workers. I asked them at one point why they thought there had been a rise in depression in recent years. Following group discussion the most common response, from men and women alike, was to say 'because you're never good enough, you never have enough and you never get there.' A viewpoint shared by the folk who attended Tim Kasser's event in Glasgow on that cold, wet December evening.

CHAPTER TWO
Why we buy

Why do people mortgage themselves to the hilt or get into serious debt so that they can have a big house with three bathrooms, fancy cars, expensive wrist watches, or a second home or yacht they never have time to use. Oliver James may attribute this to a serious dose of 'affluenza' but the economist Robert Frank calls it 'luxury fever'. And like any fever it undermines our well-being. Indeed Frank tell us: 'A host of careful studies suggest that across-the-board increases in our stocks of material goods produce virtually no measurable gains in our psychological or physical well-being.'

So why do we keep consuming more and more stuff if it doesn't add to our health and happiness? Are we simply the dupes of advertising and business or is there something more at stake? Let's look at a variety of different theories on why we have become so hooked on consumption.

Lack of love
Sue Gerhardt is a British author and psychotherapist. Her recent book *The Selfish Society: How we all forgot to love one another and made money instead* (2010) is ground-breaking. She argues that the selfishness and materialism of our society is not innate but programmed into us as a result

of our upbringing. Using evidence from neuroscience Gerhardt argues that a baby's natural instinct is to connect but our society is not geared towards fulfilling this basic drive for love and affection. Instead we give children things and encourage them to find fulfillment in materialism.

Gerhardt's thesis is indeed backed by research which shows a link between feelings of insecurity and materialism. So people brought up with a lack of money are much more likely to become materialistic than those who had adequate resources in childhood. Research also shows that children whose parents divorced are likely to be more materialistic than peers from intact families; presumably the upheaval in their lives encouraged them to feel insecure. Children whose mothers did not uphold a warm, nurturing parenting style and who exerted little positive control also develop strong materialistic tendencies. In other words, children whose needs for what Kasser calls 'security, safety and sustenance' were not met by their childhood upbringing are more likely to become materialistic.

It's also worth noting that our society now puts a great emphasis on providing materially for children and babies. Indeed the baby market has boomed so much in the past few decades that it's common for grandparents to complain that their grandchildren get more stuff in their first year than their children acquired throughout their childhood. The change is not simply about the number of items now available for babies: there is a growing luxury market (think leather baby bootees, pewter cribs and luxury blankets). This is about status more than it is about babies but there's little doubt that this pattern of spending subtly affects our idea of what infants need.

Money, status and worth

Thorstein Veblen wrote one of the most enduring books on consumption, *The Theory of the Leisure Class* (1899), during a period of economic expansion in the USA but before mass consumption and advertising. Veblen used his knowledge of human societies internationally and his sociological insight to construct a powerful theory which is as relevant now as it was a century ago.

Veblen argues that 'a leisure class' develops in societies with private property and that once individuals possess goods they are in competition with one another. The power of wealth and private goods is not their intrinsic value (food, shelter, security) though they can confer some advantages. No, what is significant about wealth and possessions is that they 'confer honour' on the basis of 'an invidious distinction'. Veblen's argument is that wealth and property originally signified prowess and efficiency but soon became a way to show the owner's moral value. So 'invidious distinction' means 'the process of valuation of persons in respect of worth'.

Once this way of measuring worth took hold then several things automatically flowed from it. It's no good possessing wealth if you do not let people know you have it. Thus the wealthy indulge in what Veblen calls 'conspicuous consumption' pouring their money into mansions and buying goods such as fancy jewellery or cutlery for no other reason than the display of wealth. People also demonstrate how much money they possess by avoiding involvement in production or work – hence the British ruling class's dislike of those who made their money through 'trade'. This also helps us to understand why the moneyed class of old spent time studying arcane subjects and adopting elaborate manners and customs.

Wearing clothes which are totally impractical for normal living and working is another way to display wealth.

Veblen calls this pattern of consumption 'wasteful' because it does 'not serve human life or human well-being'. Sadly it's an ethic which begins to permeate society. Veblen argues that the pattern of consumption of the leisured, moneyed class sets the standard for others to emulate. The higher in the social order a person is the more he or she attempts to emulate the lifestyle of the wealthy elite. This means that as the economy expanded and people had more money their lives have not 'slackened to a more comfortable pace' with continued reductions in working hours. Rather people are on a treadmill of 'conspicuous expenditure' which does not serve their long term interests or well-being.

Social comparison
Economists have also reflected for years on people's motivation to earn and to consume. In recent times they have been particularly keen to explain why western societies have not become happier as a result of becoming wealthier. A common explanation is that we are social creatures who continually compare themselves to others in order to rate how they are doing in life. Researchers have found that a majority of Americans would prefer to have less money (i.e. purchasing power) as long as it was more than others. In short, money is more about status for people than it is about what they can do with it. In effect, people are on a 'social treadmill' – they aim to become wealthier in life but if everyone else becomes equally rich then there's no satisfaction to be gained from their rising income. The economist Robert Frank argues this desire to 'keep up with the Joneses' has less to do with advertising and more to do with our immediate social and family circle.

As the American essayist H L Mencken once remarked 'wealth is having at least one hundred dollars more a year than the income of one's wife's sister's husband.'

As the economy expanded in recent decades rising consumption has become an arms race forcing people to try to keep up, not just for status reasons but because they may genuinely lose out if they don't. Frank argues: 'If I buy a custom-tailored suit for my job interview, I reduce the likelihood that others will land the same job; and in the process, I create an incentive for them to spend more than they have planned on their own interview suits.'

This argument applies to lots of things – present giving, face lifts, staying late in the office, standing up at a concert, children's birthday parties, entertaining. Since these things mostly involve money, 'individual spending decisions are the seeds of a contagious process.' Indeed Frank argues that this type of spending is completely counterproductive to our well-being; that people work long hours and spend money on things they don't need and that they would be happier if governments used economic measures (such as a progressive consumption tax) to cure luxury fever.

The rise of consumer capitalism
Other theorists do not start with basic human psychology and status differences to explain the rise of consumer culture and devote their attention to economic structures. One of the first thinkers to link consumerism with the development of American capitalism is Professor Stuart Ewen who is primarily concerned with the origins of consumer culture.

Until the 1920s, much of American life was dominated by mass production and a huge percentage of the labour force worked long hours for subsistence wages. Traditionally factories produced items for the middle and upper classes but with new techniques boosting production business leaders became concerned about 'overproduction'. To avoid the dangers of having surplus stock they needed to grow the market for goods by allowing the working class to have more buying power and leisure time.

For this expansion of the market to be successful, workers needed to be 'consumerized' – to have some improvement in their pay and more free time to spend their wages. They also needed to be persuaded to buy. Up till then working people only bought what they needed and could afford. Now they were encouraged to think beyond need to 'desires' and 'wants' and to abandon thrift.

Mass advertising was one of the main catalysts for such a transformative change. This burgeoned in the US during the 1920s, becoming a major sector of the economy. To help devise methods for mass persuasion, advertisers turned to psychologists. The approach basically involved encouraging people to feel dissatisfied with themselves and to become preoccupied by how they were seen through others' eyes. 'The notion of the individual as the object of continual and harsh social scrutiny,' writes Ewen 'underscored the arguments of much of the ad texts. . .'

While many of the advertising techniques were developed in the 1920s, as a result of the 1929 crash, the Great Depression and then World War II, the economy was not favourable to increasing consumerism. That had to wait until the 1950s' economic expansion. Then, thanks to the advent of television, adverts were able to transform 'living rooms into salesrooms'.

Central to many cultural critiques of America in the 1950s and early 60s is that it became a 'mass society' where choice, conformity and individuality were repressed as advertisers encouraged people to equate consumption with social acceptability:

> The control of the masses required that people, like the world they inhabited, assume the character of machinery – predictable and without any aspiration to self-determination. As the industrial machinery produced standardised goods, so did the psychology of consumerisation attempt to forge a notion of the "mass" as "practically identical in all mental and social characteristics".

Freud's nephew, Edward Bernays, was one of the thinkers who was keen to understand and use 'mass psychology'. He wrote: 'If we understand the mechanism and motives of the group mind, it is now possible to control and regiment the masses according to our will without their knowing it. . .' By 'our will' he meant the business and political elite. Fears of the unruly masses, attracted to destructive, irrational behaviour and easily drawn to take part in fascist or socialist movements, led many political figures and thinkers to see the encouragement of individual desires to consume as the recipe for a safer political environment.

Psychoanalytic methods to control the minds of ordinary Americans also became popular in the 50s and 60s. Clinics opened in many local neighbourhoods and the emphasis was on adhering to rigid social rules. However, by the time the 60s dawned various thinkers were challenging the control exerted by business and psychology. For example, the journalist and social critic, Vance Packard published *The*

Hidden Persuaders (1957) which was a hugely influential book alerting Americans to the manipulation in advertising and the use of planned obsolescence. In *One Dimensional Man* (1964) Herbert Marcuse argued that the capitalist economic system was leading to alienation and widespread oppression and was particularly critical of consumerism.

By the 1960s there was a growing concern in America (even in the public at large) that mass, consumer society was conformist and repressive and at odds with individual expression and freedom. The argument ran that Americans, once proud individualists and pioneers, were now 'faceless cogs in a great machine of automation' – working in oppressive organisations and living in monotonous suburbs.

Conformity, creativity and capitalism
But should we equate consumerism with conformity and see this as an essential feature of capitalist society? This may seem a pedestrian question but the answer is important to our interpretation of what happened next.

If we see consumerism and capitalism as largely about conformity then the youth and feminist rebellions from the mid 1960s on can be seen as a legitimate attempt to break free from alienation and the stultifying restraint encouraged by advertising and mass production. Indeed the cultural critic Thomas Frank and others argue that the 'standard story' puts the blame for American conformity on business and their practices and sees the ensuing 'counterculture' as liberating.

This term comes from the historian Theodore Roszak's classic text *The Making of a Counterculture* (1969). Roszak argues that all aspects of modern society including education and leisure have come to be dominated by an elite from corporate, political and scientific life and that the USA had become 'a technocracy'. Since the basic values of the system are so corrupt Roszak argues that change will only come from a seismic shift in culture and not from tinkering with the system. Thus the real change agents are not trade unionists or political activists seeking reforms but those who reject the basic values and ways of operating of a technocratic society. Indeed he argues that a revolution will come about through the lifestyle changes and personal protests of a wide range of radicals such as hippies, student protestors, feminists, war protestors, drug takers and mystics.

Charles Rich added another dimension to this analysis in his seminal work *The Greening of America* (1970). He claimed that a new consciousness based on freedom, recreational drugs and genuine equality was emerging from these protest movements and challenging the fundamental precepts of a rigidly structured society dominated by personal success and consumption. In short, this new consciousness was about liberation from oppression and the establishment's values.

More than forty years on we can see that this analysis must be flawed. Despite the plethora of movements involved in the counterculture project, and the countless millions embroiled, their thinking and action have not dented the system at all. Indeed, if anything, it's more powerful than it was in the 1960s. One explanation is that while these protest movements initially posed a threat to corporate America, business embarked on 'co-optation'. In short, business ultimately embraced and commercialised these values. So, for example, once the 'women's lib' movement made its presence felt advertisers were soon producing adverts aimed at the independent woman. Indeed in the late 1960s one senior advertising woman posed her colleagues this rhetorical question: 'Isn't this new woman, this free and loving-every-minute-of-it woman, the heavy user every industry must find and cultivate and multiply?' Liberated women like myself in the 1960s and 70s were more likely to spend money on ourselves than our much more restrained mothers. What's more, it also wasn't long before business was selling Che Guevera mugs and T-shirts, native American dream catchers or a whole raft of organic products. In other words, corporate America was soon using the symbols of counterculture to sell conventional products or designing products to appeal to various types of 'counterculturals'. As early as 1968 the mega corporation AT&T used 'The Times They Are A-Changin'' as a slogan.

The first challenge to the 'co-optation' thesis came from Thomas Frank in *The Conquest of Cool* (1997) which studied the evolution of 'business thought' in the USA. Frank argues that before the countercultural movement ever appeared on the scene, business – particularly in the advertising sector – was already alive with new thinking and were rebelling against the inflexibility and conformity of American business practices encouraged by 'Taylorism'. They were in the process of transforming their organisations to encourage more flexibility and creativity. Advertisers were also beginning to turn their attention to youth as there was huge economic potential inherent in the bulging baby boomer generation.

So, according to Frank, business in America quickly embraced the countercultural movement because they had a strong sense of 'kinship'. 'Hip capitalism wasn't something on the fringes of enterprise, an occasional hippie entrepreneur selling posters or drug paraphernalia,' he writes. 'Nor was it a purely demographic manoeuvre. . . What happened in the sixties is that hip became central to the way that American capitalism understood itself and explained itself to the public.'

Rebellion™

Frank's compelling argument was taken much further by two Canadian academics – Joseph Heath and Andrew Potter – in their challenging book *The Rebel Sell* (2005).

Heath and Potter take a left-wing perspective but do not buy into the idea that consumer desires are simply the result of advertising or a corporate plot. They follow Veblen in arguing that people do not simply consume to feel that they are just like everyone else but to prove their worth, advance in the social hierarchy and feel 'distinctive'.

The old way of achieving distinction was via class which had embedded within it notions of 'good taste'. Indeed the whole class system, even in the USA, was modelled on the values and character of the English aristocracy. This 'bourgeois' value system always had its opponents, most notably 'the bohemians' who valued individual self-expression. This can be thought of as an opposition of 'square' and 'hip' values. Heath and Potter argue that the counter-culture movement had such a profound effect on the dominant status system, not by completely eliminating the class system and bourgeois (square) values (they are still there) but by ensuring that 'cool . . . usurped class as the dominant status system in America.'

However, this takeover of hip, cool, bohemian values did not challenge American capitalism – it invigorated it. Bourgeois values may prize materialism and possessions but they also value 'order, regularity, custom, rational thinking, self-discipline, and productivity'. The countercultural values by contrast are about individuality, self-expression, creativity, novelty, rebellion. . . In short, they are not antithetical to capitalism; they are more in tune with the relentless pursuit of new markets than bourgeois values ever were. 'It is true that genuine creativity is completely rebellious and subversive, since it disrupts existing patterns of thought and life, ' Heath and Potter write. But they add: 'It subverts everything *except capitalism itself*.' After all, in the words of Joseph Schumpeter the essential fact about capitalism is that it is based on the process of 'creative destruction'.

The essence of cool

Let's look in more depth at what it means to be 'cool'. Heath and Potter don't think this is essentially about real individuality since if people want to be genuinely different then they can simply behave erratically. No, individuals show that they are cool by making sure that they're on the right side of cool v. square which has an 'either/or' feel to it. The novelist Norman Mailer set out his distinction between being 'hip and 'square' in 1959. Some of the words he associated with *hip* are nihilistic, self, body, anarchists and marijuana whereas the equivalents for *square* are authoritarian, society, mind, socialists, salvation and alcohol. Heath and Potter write, 'The superficialities of fashion may change but the deep structure of cool as rebellious non conformity provides us with a surprisingly stable and enduring set of guidelines.' It's worth noting that Mailer was writing at the end of the 1950s when radical political action in the USA was dangerous as radicals risked being denounced as communist and being charged or losing their jobs. No wonder youth rebellion was channelled into essentially hedonistic behaviour.

This enduring definition of hip and cool is ultra individualistic. It easily encourages a narcissistic self-focus which not only impedes the formation of good personal relationships but also lionises anti-social attitudes and bad behaviour. Anything that looks like a restriction on the individual's freedom 'sucks'. Unfortunately the rules of civility and politeness which once governed social interaction are now seen as square and old-fashioned and an unnecessary infringement on an individual's authentic self-expression.

Such a philosophy is bound to suck the life out of conventional forms of politics and political action as they are judged to be part of a corrupt and repressive system as well as being boring and square. Even radicals see change as essentially about individuals and their personal growth and transformation in lifestyles. Issues of equality, fairness and social justice – once the primary concern of progressives in America as elsewhere – were jettisoned to make way for much more business-oriented and self-serving concerns.

The American dream

When I started writing this chapter I did not intend to focus on America and yet its history and thinkers inveigled their way onto these pages. And they belong there. America is the land of supersized consumption. When it comes to materialism they have taken the lead and other countries, like our own, have blithely followed. What's more, since the UK is dominated by American media, we know their story. Can we not picture in our minds the American movies and TV series which exemplify these various theories?

CHAPTER THREE

Generation We to 'Generation Me'

It would be easy to make the media, politics, economics and social trends the focus of this book, filling the pages with data on materialism's increasing stranglehold on our lives. But this book is about people – how we see ourselves, our relationships, our hopes and fears, how we try to find meaning and purpose in our lives and the type of society we inhabit. In short, this book is about the stuff of everyday life.

It would also be easy for me, an intellectual woman living in comfortable circumstances, to forget how beneficial material advancement has been to people's lives. So, for both these reasons, I commence this chapter by looking at one older woman's story.

The older generation – a positive story

My mother was born in 1921, orphaned at an early age, and grew up in Milngavie mainly with her grandmother. Life was challenging and she describes her early life as 'quite poor'. Though she quickly adds that there was nothing unusual about this as all their neighbours had a similar standard of living. In those days houses were typically small – many families lived in one or two rooms – and were plainly furnished. Indeed my mother recalls that working people really did not strive to do much with their homes and variation in houses was not about décor or possessions but simply about how clean and orderly they were.

When my mother was young, children spent most of their non-school time outdoors: toys and things hardly featured in their lives. They usually played in large groups comprising children of all ages. The games – such as hide and seek, kick-the-can, whips and peeries, beds and skipping ropes – were mainly physical and required, at most, basic equipment. Again children hardly varied in their access to toys or the where-withal for games. The same was true of clothes and shoes.

Apart from the church and school, what were the external influences on their young minds? A few comics, a few newspapers and a few books. My mother did not listen to radio regularly until she was well into her 20s but she more than made up for the lack of radio listening with cinema going. Indeed she remembers going to the cinema three times a week throughout her teens and twenties which meant that she saw every new film shown in her local picture house. She was not alone: Scotland as a whole, but particularly Glasgow and its hinterland, was cinema daft. At least they liked American films, not British ones which were considered 'duff'.

As I argue in my book on Glasgow, *The Tears that Made the Clyde* (2010), the pub and football were men's great escape from hard working conditions and cramped overcrowded living conditions. The cinema and dancing were women's equivalent and they helped to make up for the dreariness and drudgery of women's lives. There's little doubt that life was particularly hard for young working class women in those times. I literally feel exhausted when my mother tells me about the job she had in the laundry in Milngavie from when she left school at 14 until she left to get married 13 years later. Not only were the working hours long (8 till 6 and a half day on a Saturday) but standing in a hot, steamy atmosphere shaking out sheets or using mangles and wringers was back-breaking work.

No wonder she was keen to go to the cinema three nights a week. She is clear that its main attraction was 'escapism' – it was wonderful to sit there admiring the good looks, clothes and surroundings of these American idols. 'Didn't you want to be like them?', I ask her but she does not entertain the proposition. These film stars' lives were so far removed from hers it didn't make sense to think she could copy them. Besides, people didn't have the time, money or even access to clothes to make copying at all viable. Except in hairstyles.

When I quiz her further on what access to glamour she and her friends had I am struck by how limited it was – how different from today's generation. Of course, they wanted to look their best but they didn't have many tools at their disposal. They only had a few outfits and face powder and lipstick. Beauty products consisted of little more than soap and water, cold cream and a pair of tweezers – items generally bought in Woolworths. As there were no adverts in the cinema, no television and little exposure to magazines other than *My Weekly* and *The People's Friend,* folk like my mother generally didn't feel deprived of things they couldn't afford. Indeed my mother claims that she would only know about things to buy because she saw them in the shops.

The benefits of consumer goods

When rationing stopped and the economy benefited from the birth of the baby boomers in the 1950s, consumer goods became more widely available. New housewives and mothers in the late 1940s and 50s now hankered after various 'mod cons' – washing machines, fridges, vacuum cleaners and later telephones. These were items which made a welcome difference to women's lives saving them the drudgery of whole days washing or hours spent on daily outings to the shops. I can still remember vividly the day our family became the proud possessor of a washing machine. Much of this was about the pleasure of anticipation. Until recent times ordinary people couldn't indulge in 'immediate gratification' as they couldn't afford to. What's more, as there was no hire purchase folk had to save up to buy more expensive items. Because things were scarce they were looked after and savoured. Paradoxically people enjoy things more when they have less.

My mother easily recalls how fitted carpets, immersion heaters and later central heating meant that life became much more comfortable. We lived in a new 1950s council house and until we got storage heaters in the 60s it was freezing: we huddled over the coal fire and dressed in front of the gas oven. Every winter would see a predictable round of chilblains on fingers and toes.

But by far the biggest change that came about as a result of the economic expansion was mass access to television. The BBC had started in 1936 but it wasn't until 1952 that TV broadcasting resumed and ordinary working people started to own their own sets. We got ours in 1955 (in a walnut cabinet) just in time for the beginning of ITV and commercial television. The Scots loved it. Indeed TV proved so popular that by the early 60s the number of cinemas in Scotland had halved.

My mother is extremely positive about the benefits of modernity and it's easy to see why. In her lifetime she has gone from living in physically cold and bleak circumstances which often demanded real hard labour to a life of relative ease and affluence. She loves her central heating and she likes buying things for her house though she rarely replaces anything unless it's worn or broken. She likes watching television and one of her favourite pastimes is going to the shops. She still buys a few clothes and gets her hair done regularly but she is not particularly conscious of her appearance and would never compare herself to others or try to be something she's not. My mother has had the best of materialism. Like many of her generation she's one of the lucky ones.

The resilience of the older generation

I am won over by the argument that statistics on the level of depression in some Western societies, particularly the USA, are inflated as doctors, and the public at large, do not make an adequate distinction between sadness (a normal human response to loss) and 'depression' which implies a mental disorder. But depression has risen so much in the past few decades that it's impossible to believe that this is all down to definition. Some of it must be about changing life circumstances. Writing in 1990 on a large study of Americans, Professor Martin Seligman pointed out that 6 per cent of 18-24 year-olds and 9 per cent of 25-44 year olds reported depression whereas the figure for the over-65s was only 1 per cent even though they had lived more years in which they could have succumbed. Seligman considers various explanations such as memory and willingness to admit problems but concludes by saying, 'I lean strongly to the possibility that people born later in this [twentieth] century have actually experienced much more depression than those born earlier.'

Looking at the story of the older generation it's easy to see why they were less likely to suffer depression as their personal circumstances fostered perseverance, acceptance and appreciation of the small things in life – key aspects of resilience. What's more, the absence of media in their lives (other than escapist cinema which they saw as fantasy) allowed this generation to develop their own personalities.

Interestingly this is the conclusion reached by English schoolgirls involved in a local history project in Preston. The project called Lessons from the Past (2011) involved interviews with fifty local women who reminisced about their lives from as early as 1915. What struck the girls most forcibly is that the pre-war generation of women had lived much better lives than they had expected. They anticipated that women of this time would have been hampered by low expectations, traditional roles and limitations on their freedoms. The girls had explicitly thought that the absence of positive role models for these women would have hampered their development. They were then shocked to find themselves speculating that the *absence* of any type of role model had been a boon to these older women. 'It became clear that what the older women had was a good understanding of who they were and what they wanted and liked,' they write, adding, 'they knew their strengths and weaknesses and never felt the need to change either.' In short, these older women had the confidence to be themselves in both personality and appearance.

What I've noticed about women of my mother's generation is that they attribute good looks, or cleverness, to 'the luck of the draw'. They took a matter-of-fact view of themselves which allowed them to say that they had been blessed in life by good legs or figure but that they didn't have great hair or skin. They did their best to make up for weaknesses but they ultimately accepted the way they were. This outlook on life made it easier to accept that your appearance inevitably got worse as you aged.

One of the Preston girls' main conclusions from their research is that there had been a 'deterioration' of women through the generations. It certainly appears that the generation younger than my mother (those in their 70s and 80s), who grew up with much more media exposure, are much more likely to fall victim to anxieties about body image and even 'body dysmorphic disorder'. Dr Alex Yellowlees is a consultant psychiatrist in Glasgow and he believes that body dissatisfaction now affects both young and old. He tells us:

> It was once the case that we were happy to coast
> into retirement and relax in old age, but now even
> in these later stages of life I am seeing people who
> are pre-occupied with shape, weight and looks in a
> way that was once the domain of younger people
> who had yet to find their path or identity in life.

Indeed Dr Yellowlees reports a worrying rise in older patients suffering from eating disorders as they attempt to achieve what he refers to as 'an unrealistic physical ideal'.

It's worth noting that UK consumers spent £2.3 bn in 2010 on cosmetic surgery and that the number of procedures continues to rise despite the recession. No part of the body seems immune to criticism or the desire for improvement.

There is a huge rise in the number of women undergoing cosmetic surgery on their genitals. In the USA the latest trend is foot surgery to facilitate the wearing of high heels.

Today's generation and looks

Given the fact that our society is increasingly concerned with appearance it is hardly surprising that if you talk to teachers and youth workers these days they will report their concern that girls, from even a young age, are becoming increasingly obsessed with, and critical of, how they look. These professionals fear this is damaging the girls' self-esteem. This message came over so loudly to two MPs – Jo Swinson and Lynne Featherstone – when they were consulting youth groups that they set up the 'Campaign for Body Confidence'. Their main focus has been the size of models and how airbrushed images are now so common it's giving a false perception of what real people look like.

Survey after survey is now picking up how much young people are critical of their appearance. For example, research has found that 40 per cent of teenage girls say that they have considered plastic surgery. Research published in the *British Journal of Developmental Psychology* found that 71 per cent of 7 year-olds want to be thinner with many saying that it would make them more popular. Another study found that half of girls aged 14 say it's important to be attractive to boys – 50 per cent higher than it was ten years ago. A similar rise can be seen in boys.

At every turn girls are subjected to glamorous images – either the voluptuous, successful women in raunchy music videos or the unhealthily skinny models in the fashion magazines.

Educational psychologists and teachers report a rise in 'fashion bullying' where young people are picked on for their clothes or other aspects of their appearance. This issue found its way onto newspapers' front pages recently as a 14 year old boarding school girl with bulimia hanged herself as she could not stand being taunted by other girls for her size. (She was actually very slight.) Rightly or wrongly, the coroner blamed the fashion industry's obsession with 'wafer-thin' models for her death.

One college lecturer at one of our events recently reported that she feels she belongs to a completely different generation from the young women in their late teens that she teaches: many of them admit to spending three hours every morning getting ready to go to college. It's not surprising – fake tans, hair extensions, false nails and elaborate make-up routines absorb time. For decades, if not millennia, girls preened themselves for special occasions but nowadays vulnerable girls have so much invested in their appearance that they dare not go out unless they are looking their best. Just think how they could spend that time.

Another cause for concern is the young age at which girls now become interested in cosmetics, clothes and their appearance. Girls as young as six go to make-up parties; young girls under ten are being treated to an all-over fake tan; primary, not just secondary, pupils commonly attend hugely expensive proms involving trips to hairdressers and beauticians as well as fancy dresses and stretch limousines.

The rise of 'Generation Me'

It's worth pointing out that some researchers, most notably the distinguished political scientist Ronald Inglehart, refer to the older generation as 'materialist' and the younger generation as 'post-materialist'. This very influential argument, based on considerable international research, is that the generation born before World War II were mainly concerned about security and economic matters such as wages and prices whereas the younger generation are much more interested in political liberties, autonomy and self-expression. But this is a very skewed perspective on the older generation whose philosophy of life stressed prudence, thrift and restraint. Indeed, as many commentators have pointed out, in response to Inglehart's research, the materialist vs. post-materialist nomenclature hardly makes sense given that consumerism has burgeoned in recent times.

The older generation's emphasis on deferred gratification, living within your means, and 'make do and mend' was an understandable response to tough living conditions engendered by lack of resources, insecurity and the ravages and shortages created by world wars. But it was also a practical philosophy of life reinforced by proverbs and sayings embodying folk wisdom, and the teachings of the church.

At the core of this older way of life is the notion that other people matter as much as you and should be respected. This is why it was commonplace for mothers and fathers to sacrifice their own needs and wants for their families. Good manners and politeness also mattered and while many now mock such traditions often all they involved was taking into consideration other people's feelings and needs – not just your own.

Taking others' needs into account had community benefits as well. This philosophy of life emphasised neighbourliness and accepting restrictions on your own freedom or comfort for other people's benefit – a clear contrast to the nimbyism of our own times. Until the 1970s the UK's political culture was for centuries dominated by issues of fairness, equality and justice. Even that entrepreneurial firebrand and self-made man Andrew Carnegie argued passionately that 'the man who dies rich dies disgraced'. By producing figures such as Robert Burns, Keir Hardie and Jimmy Maxton Scotland played an important part in enunciating these humanitarian or socialist ideals.

Looking back it's easy to believe that politicians like Maxton were marginal and irrelevant as they never won outright political power yet much of what they argued for – decent housing, a proper safety-net and free health care – has come about as a result of the mainstreaming of these once radical ideas.

It's wrong to believe that life was uniformly better in the old days: there were strong pressures to conform and homophobia, racism, sexism and sectarianism were rife. People with disabilities were mocked and often marginalised. Those who wanted something more from life often had to emigrate as they could see little opportunity for development of any kind within their homeland.

Some thinkers argue that people are by nature selfish and motivated by their own survival. I don't accept this viewpoint and am much more inclined to uphold the idea that we are motivated by 'reciprocal altruism'. However, even if we accept a Darwinian viewpoint it's easy to see how that older philosophy of life, emanating from tough economic circumstances, the church and politics, tempered and reined in selfishness and acquisitiveness. The decline of religion, the loosening of family and community bonds and the erosion of socialist idealism meant that there was no counterweight to the rise of acquisitive individualism encouraged by the rise of mass marketing and consumerism.

Life has changed substantially in this respect since the 1950s. Ours is now an age which encourages pleasure-seeking not restraint and debt over delayed gratification. At every turn people are encouraged to focus on the self rather than others and on their individual freedom rather than community cohesion or well-being. Shopping is the new religion and advertising and canned, mass entertainment provides its liturgy.

We are much richer than in my mother's formative days, but we are beset by chronic and apparently unsolvable problems ranging from climate change, huge public debt and how people will be gainfully employed. Rates of happiness have hardly budged since the 1950s and rates of suicide and mental illness have risen steeply.

Inglehart calls my mother's generation 'materialist' because they inhabited an economically insecure world which made them focus on money and how they could feed, house and buy basic goods such as shoes for their children. The younger generation may not be materialistic in this way but money, clothes and gadgets are crucially important to their lives. For them a pair of shoes is not about protecting the feet but about showing you are 'cool' or belong to the right group: shoes are about social acceptability and feelings of self-esteem.

Since the 1970s American culture has been dominated by the supposed importance of self-esteem and they have exported these ideas to other English speaking cultures via the mass media. Self-esteem is a pleasant feeling but its exponents have exaggerated its benefits. Indeed their message is akin to saying that the only nutrient that matters is vitamin C and that we all require constant, artificial doses.

Decades ago child psychologists in the USA warned that educational and child-rearing practices which encouraged the child to focus on his or her feelings and to believe that they were 'special' were not going to boost self-esteem – they were going to develop narcissism. And it appears that they were right as narcissistic personality disorders have risen in the USA in recent years.

It's hardly surprising that Jean Twenge, an American psychologist who has made a study of young people's attitudes and how they have evolved over the past fifty years, entitled her book *Generation Me* (2006).

Professor Martin Seligman, one of the world's leading psychologists, believes that such child-rearing practices undermine resilience and set children up for depression by encouraging them to blow out of all proportion any set-back they have in life or any negative feelings. But he also argues that modern culture as a whole encourages 'the bloated self' which is obsessed with its own life, feelings and doings. It's this self-obsession which he thinks undermines people's sense of meaning and purpose as, by definition, meaning is about serving a goal larger than yourself. This has real life consequences as people who lack a sense of meaning are vulnerable to depression. From this perspective our grannies' mantra – 'yer no the centre of the universe' – may be a better, and more fulfilling way to live your life than thinking that the world revolves round you.

Every great world religion has the inherent notion that to live a good life, to encounter the divine or to experience contentment, people need to find ways to sidestep or reduce the ego. There's general acceptance that spiritual feelings are about feeling a small part of a large, infinite whole. Spirituality is about a sense of connection. This is why even non-religious experiences such as gazing at the sky on a starry night, standing on a mountain top, listening to a choir sing or even being part of a large crowd often lead to spiritual feelings as they provoke that sense of smallness and connection. By contrast Americanised Western culture is fixated with developing and boosting the ego which is likely to undermine contentment and lead to feelings of disconnection.

Over thirty years ago an American historian, Christopher Lasch, wrote a seminal book called *The Culture of Narcissism* (1979). In it he lays out how various developments were conspiring to create a narcissistic culture. He specifically blamed the right's increasing promotion of the individual and the free market as well as the moral laxity of the left, which encouraged individualism by weakening links to family and community. In other words, obsession with ourselves and others' approval was now the focus of people's lives.

If anything Lasch underestimated this crucial change in culture. If we add in to his diagnosis the current media's fixations, influence and reach then we have 'the perfect storm' – narcissism with knobs on.

CHAPTER FOUR

The opium of the people

Here's a snippet from a conversation between two men in one of Glasgow's poor housing estates:

1st man: See doctors, they get 120,000 quid a year.

2nd man: 120,000! Makes you wonder how many plasma tellies they've got.

Television is at the heart of ordinary people's culture in the UK. In fact, it *is* ordinary folk's culture. People on average watch four hours per day of real time (i.e. not recorded) TV and the set is switched on in the average house for over six hours per day. Remember these are averages: there's a sizeable number of people who watch in excess of seven hours per day. In some homes the telly is never switched off and all meals are taken sitting in front of 'the box'.

Viewing figures are even higher in Scotland – four and a half hours a day – nearing American figures. Unlike a few decades ago when households only had one set and viewing was communal, now the average UK household possesses 2.6 sets – one for each person. As the Glaswegian above demonstrates, in popular culture the quantity and quality of sets is a good marker of social status and success.

There are lots of excellent programmes to watch on television. TV can entertain, educate, broaden the mind and aid relaxation. As people are always telling me, it can be a great comfort to older folk who live on their own. But television is not only a major conduit for unhealthy materialist values, people's television viewing habits can have a profoundly negative effect on their well-being and social life.

Television – a suitable case for treatment?
Over a century ago Karl Marx called religion 'the opium of the people'. If he were alive today he would make this judgement about television. However, the parallel between opium and TV is not simply that it sedates and promotes acceptance; like opium, but unlike religion, television is addictive – not physically but behaviourally.

'Television addiction is no mere metaphor' is the title of an article co-authored by Milhaly Csikszentmihalyi – one of the world's leading psychologists. The authors accept that some television viewing can enhance people's lives if they view selectively and for short periods. However, given the level of television viewing and the fact that, after sleep and work, it absorbs more time than any other activity, then the majority are more likely to find television damaging rather than beneficial. When interviewed, heavy television viewers often express a frustration with how much time they spend watching it and at least 10 per cent describe themselves as 'addicted'.

The definition of substance abuse used by psychologists and psychiatrists includes the following criteria: 'spending a great deal of time using the substance; using it more often than one intends; thinking about reducing use or making repeated unsuccessful efforts to reduce use; giving up important social, family and occupational activities to use it; and reporting withdrawal symptoms when one stops using it.' This describes even average users of television given that they're watching for around four hours per day and giving up the opportunity to do other things with their time.

Part of the explanation for TV's addictive quality is what's termed our biological 'orienting response'. As human beings we have an instinctive response to novel auditory and visual stimuli. This is one of the reasons why it's often impossible to avert our eyes from a blinking television set. Watching TV is also pleasurable. It can help relax and distract the brain after a day's hard work which probably explains why so many people slump in front of the TV if they're feeling stressed and tired. Other researchers argue that TV appeals to our basic human interest in other people.

But viewers pay a hefty price for these benefits. Television viewing is a passive activity. Indeed one researcher into television's effects, argues that 'television viewing is not an "experience".' Rather it replaces experience. Television viewing, unlike other activities such as hobbies, sports, social- ising and reading, lowers people's mood, making them feel apathetic and drained of energy. Research has also shown that TV viewers become 'less creative in problem solving, less able to persevere at tasks and less tolerant of unstructured time.' This can easily set up a vicious circle: people watch increasing amounts of television because they become progr- essively unable to do anything else.

Clearly television use can undermine health. Heavy users are more likely to be obese and unlikely to participate in sporting or community activities. Indeed researchers have shown that as television came into people's lives their participation in the community collapsed. This is one of the reasons why older people need to use television for company. Robert Putnam, author of that international best-seller *Bowling Alone* (2000), argues that the easiest way for people to build community is to 'turn off the TV' as '. . . the more entertainment television you watch, the less civically engaged you are. People watch *Friends* rather than having friends.'

The impact of media advertising

Some experts and critics argue that advertising drives a great deal of consumption. 'Advertisers have programmed many of us into a shopping habit,' writes one mass media expert. From the birth of the industry in the USA, advertisers have relied on psychologists to help them create and influence people's desires. For example, psychologists suggested that they should convince people that what they owned was inferior and required upgrading to make them socially acceptable. It's worth noting that for over a hundred years America has spent around 2 per cent of its GDP on advertising. The UK and other Anglo-American countries spend about 1 per cent and European countries about half of this amount.

Over the years various commentators have blamed advertising for anything they dislike about consumer culture but it is, of course, much more complicated than this. Indeed Veblen's ideas on conspicuous consumption are important because they show that even without advertising we are drawn to buy, not because of need, but to give us worth and distinction.

What advertising does is encourage these basic drives and, by directing our attention to specific products gives them status through prominence and repeated exposure. The effect of advertising is subtle. In the words of two advertising analysts: 'We are just not aware of the small differences advertising can make. Even though these imperceptibly small changes in time add up to significant effects, individual increments are too small for us to notice.' People rarely feel the need to buy as the result of seeing one single advert so remain blissfully unaware of the cumulative effect.

What's more, because we are now exposed to so many adverts, businesses have come to devote considerable time and money to advertising their brands rather than specific products. Apple and Nike are good examples of iconic, global brands which have managed to convey their 'brand values' via distinctive logos or a memorable slogan. And this is hugely powerful. By the age of 3 almost 70 per cent of children can recognise the McDonald's logo yet less than half know their own surname. By the age of 10 the average child is able to recognise almost 400 brand names.

As repetition matters, television is an ideal medium for advertising and it's getting better by the year. In 2006 UK viewers watched an average of 39 adverts a day. Now, it's 45 – almost a fifth more. This is due to rising viewing figures, the growing share of commercial TV and the fact that these channels are now allowed to pack in even more adverts.

Research confirms that television is a better method for advertising than either radio or the print media. 'We found that television is indeed a particularly effective communication medium for transmitting core information,' writes one researcher, 'because it can split the message between speech and image, in the form of iconic gestures' – an 'extremely effective mode of communication.'

The advertising industry maintains that adverts do not increase consumption (market size) and simply affect the share of the market by different companies or brands. But this defies common sense and is challenged by various researchers. Indeed one recent study:

> . . . presents evidence that advertising increases overall consumption; that it promotes and normalises a whole host of behaviours, attitudes and values, many of which are socially and environmentally damaging; that it manipulates individuals on a subconscious level, both children and adults; and that it is so pervasive in modern society as to make the choice of opting-out from exposure virtually impossible.

Of most relevance to our study are the values adverts convey and how they influence people's feelings and desires. Given the brevity of this book I'm not going to spend time convincing readers of something they already know: a great deal of advertising is not selling products but aspirations and dreams. For example, by associating brown bread with family life and security an advert can encourage us to believe that we could experience these positive things too if we bought that loaf. This is fanciful and breeds discontent but it's not as cynical as some of the techniques advertisers employ.

One of the differences between old-fashioned and modern methods of advertising (i.e. post 1920) is the attempt to 'turn the consumer's critical functions away from the product and toward himself.' Advertisers deliberately aimed to make people discontented not just with their environment and what they owned but with themselves as people. And they were explicit about this. For example, writing in the advertisers' house journal in the USA one commentator urged ad men to make people 'self-conscious about matter of course things such as enlarged nose pores, bad breath. . .' A 1920s Cutex magazine advert told women: 'You will be amazed to find how many times in one day people glance at your nails. At each glance a judgment is made. . . Indeed some people make a practice of basing their estimate of a new acquaintance largely upon this one detail.'

Exposure to these types of messages was limited until well into the 1950s. It was more of a drip, drip, drip into people's minds – minds generally preoccupied by matters other than appearance. Fast forward to our own day and the volume of ads which come at us from different types of media – television, billboards, magazines, the internet – and we can see that the messages that we need to fix aspects of ourselves to be socially acceptable have swollen to a huge torrent.

In today's world, people – men and women – are increasingly critical about their appearance and it's simplistic to argue this is simply about TV advertising. Women's magazines also bear a great deal of responsibility: in the guise of helping women to feel good about themselves the underlying message is that they're not okay the way they are. Much of what masquerades as copy is little more than advertorial for products designed to improve readers' many imperfections.

Television programmes too are responsible for the negative way people feel about themselves and their lives. A study undertaken in the USA in the early 1980s found that as TV was gradually introduced into various states of the union their rate of 'larceny' (theft) rose. The researcher gave two plausible explanations. First television stimulates desire for the type of consumer goods seen on TV – not just in adverts but in programmes. During the 1950s working people were exposed for the first time to the lifestyle of the middle and upper classes and were encouraged to aspire to what they had. Second, these programmes encouraged working class viewers to have a sense of 'relative deprivation' so that if they could not acquire the desired goods legally or through debt (a later phenomenon) then theft was one of the few ways to obtain what they desired. All of this foreshadowed what happened on some English city streets in the riots of 2011.

Interestingly, many American 1950s and 60s TV series (which were also broadcast in the UK) were about middle-class lifestyles – for example, *I Love Lucy* or *The Mary Tyler Moore Show*. But by the 1980s and the take-off of radical, free market ideas, the programmes consumed by the masses changed too. Thus we entered the era of *Dallas*, *The Cosby Show* and *The Fresh Prince of Bel-air* which all featured the rich or the super rich.

This is not the complete picture for the UK, however. Unlike America UK channels have always shown programmes featuring ordinary working people such as *Coronation Street*, *Eastenders* or *River City*. Nonetheless the fact that these American series were hugely popular shows that we were also affected by this fascination with wealth and luxury.

Social comparison

The impact of this type of media is not simply that, alongside advertising, it encourages consumption and the adoption of materialist values: television, and the media in general, encourage us to compare ourselves with others. In *Britain on the Couch* (1998) Oliver James attributes much of the rise in depression in modern times to social comparison which he sees as a standard human activity. He argues that in 1950 the average Briton would have been able to name 400-500 people. By the 1980s this figure had doubled and would be even higher in today's world. Most of these people have been supplied by the media and they've become our reference group. So rather than comparing ourselves with others in our family, community or occupational group we are not just able, but actively encouraged, to compare ourselves with those who are exceedingly attractive, rich or successful. When we add in the fact that many of these attractive people have been enhanced artificially through air brushing, cosmetics and plastic surgery it's easy to see how unrealistic and negative these comparisons become.

Douglas Kenrick, a social psychologist, has documented just how damaging these types of 'contrast effects' can be for individuals. In his first experiment, carried out in the late 70s, Kenrick asked male students who had been watching the popular TV series, *Charlie's Angels* (starring Pamela Anderson and Farrah Fawcett Major), to rate the attractiveness of a young woman of average attractiveness. These men rated the woman as less attractive than did equivalent male students who hadn't been watching glamorous women on the television at the time of rating.

A later study showed that men who had viewed centrefolds from magazines like *Playboy* rated their own partners' attractiveness much more critically than men who had been looking at abstract art or pictures of average women. The men looking at the girlie magazines also reported loving their partners less than the men in the control group.

These researchers believe that given men's volume of exposure to glamorous women in mainstream television and advertising this has real life effects on men's relationships with women. Kenrick and other researchers have also shown that women's exposure to particularly attractive women in the media also undermines their feelings about themselves. Television tends to feature very successful men and this can also have a negative effect on how women see their much more ordinary partner. So it's unsurprising that men are not immune either from these 'contrast effects'.

This type of invidious social comparison has been amplified in recent years by television's obsession with 'make-over' programmes which invite viewers to rate their looks, figures, naked bodies, houses, gardens, cooking ability, parenting styles. . . This has all been a great boon for business but at the expense of how people feel about themselves.

Television has also helped to foster the rise of 'celebrity culture' as more programmes are about, or fronted by, a small band of people who are beautiful, famous or rich – ideally all three. Ironically 'reality TV' and talent shows have also fuelled the fixation with celebrity and fame by conveying to ordinary people that just like winning the lottery 'it could be you'. And just as a few people do win the lottery, rather than being struck by lightening, TV does make a few people into stars – Jade Goody and Scotland's own Susan Boyle being the two most iconic examples.

Of course, none of the factors covered in this chapter are on their own damaging to people. It's neither here not there if someone picks up an occasional magazine or watches a few adverts, an occasional *Big Brother* episode or *Strictly Come Dancing*.

But for an increasing number of people the media is the focus of their non work lives and how they pass the time. If people watch television for an average of four hours a day, pick up a newspaper such as *The Metro*, *The Mail* or *The Sun* a couple of times a week, read a weekly magazine such as *Grazia*, *Nuts* or *Hello*, or use the internet for entertainment, then they will be steeped in celebrity culture and they are likely to feel, albeit at an unconscious level, the full force of the media's negative effects.

The effect of computers and phones

Some readers may think that I'm out of date in concentrating on television when, in the past few years, there has also been a rise in computer use, and social networking – especially in the UK. However, there is evidence that the computer and mobile phone have not dented the amount of TV people are exposed to as they often do things like texting or tweeting while watching television.

Superficially, it appears preferable for people to use computers than watch TV as they are less passive and more in control when using the internet and social media. This may be true but there's still a hefty price. In the words of one observer: 'Whether in or out of the home, more people of *all* ages in the UK are physically and socially disengaged from the people around them because they are wearing earphones, talking or texting on a mobile telephone, or using a laptop or Blackberry.' Britons now socially interact with other people for less than 50 minutes every day. This figure has fallen dramatically in the past decades – first as a result of television use and now as a result of various kinds of electronic media.

This has big implications for health and social life. We are social creatures who need face-to-face interaction. Lots of research now shows that the more friends people have and the more time they spend with them the better their health as these social interactions can have a beneficial effect on blood pressure and the immune system, thus protecting health. Older people who spend limited time with others are more likely to suffer memory loss and dementia.

The whole world is watching

Another aspect of modern media is that it encourages people to think that one of the best things in life is to be famous – to have people watching you. An American professor Mark Crispin Miller argues, 'To be the centre of attention is a tremendous pleasure, and we've always known this. It's fun to be famous. It's fun to have people paying attention to you.' As an older Scot I don't completely agree with this statement, nonetheless I think he is right to point out that this is the ethos of the modern age. Miller also states:

> . . . since we live in a completely visual, completely spectacular culture now because of the pervasiveness of TV and the cult of celebrity, we now conceive of that kind of pleasure as the greatest good. The highest, finest thing that life has to offer is to be on TV, is to have a whole huge audience clapping for you, is to be a performer, is to win gold at the Olympics. That's it. That's the greatest pleasure.

As he goes on to point out, this mentality then encourages us to play down the pleasure to be derived from private spheres of life such as intimacy or 'using your mind, thinking your own thoughts.' Youngsters are particular casualties of this all-persuasive idea that 'the whole world is watching.'

Children and young people's use of the media

So let's move on to look at the impact of the media on children and youth. We encountered some of this in a previous chapter when we looked at children and young people's rising anxiety about their appearance. Given what we've now seen, we have a better understanding of why this has happened. Young people's exposure to the media is worrying. Almost 90 per cent of teenagers and 60 per cent of 5-6-year-olds have their own personal television, usually in their bedrooms. Around 60 per cent of youngsters watch TV before going to school, during meals and prior to sleep. The more deprived a youngster is the more these figures apply partly because the household doesn't have the resources for alternative activities. Two-thirds of those between 7 and 16 access the internet from their own bedrooms. Indeed it's important to understand that much of young people's media use is solitary.

In *Consumer Kids* (2009) the authors starkly set out how much screen time UK children are now exposed to:

> In total, children today spend an average of 5 hours and 18 minutes every single day in front of a screen. That's 2 hours 36 minutes of TV; 1 hour 18 minutes on the internet and 1 hour 24 minutes on a games console. Total screen time, then, is around 2,000 hours a year. If we consider that children aged 9 to 11 spend 900 hours in class per year and children age 6 to 12 spend an average of 3.5 hours a day with their parents (and presumably less after that age), children's time in front of a screen is more than double their time in class and more than one-and-a-half times what they spend with parents.

If anything this is an underestimate as more recent data suggests that internet use is now two hours per day and that youngsters are adept at multitasking so they are looking at a variety of screens (and therefore absorbing more adverts) at the same time.

Does all of this matter? Of course it does:

- The American Academy of Paediatrics recommends that no child under two should watch television as it may affect their developing brains. Over this age TV viewing should be limited to two hours per day.

- Videos claiming to enhance babies' cognitive development have actually been shown to retard it. Children who watch TVs and videos under two have delayed language skills.

- Since the 1950s thousands of studies have shown a link between children's exposure to violence in the media and violent behaviour (in the present and in adulthood); desensitization to violence; nightmares; fear of being attacked; and less empathy with others.

- TV viewing can lead to sleep problems and disorders in children and adolescents particularly if they have a television in their bedrooms. Lack of sleep is associated with a number of psychological and physiological problems.

- The more television a child watches the more likely he/she is to be overweight, eat unhealthily and have health problems such as cardiovascular disease and type 2 diabetes.

- Some experts claim that the effects on the brain of repeated computer game use resemble the effects of substance misuse.

These concerns are additional to the problems created by

commercial pressures and exposure to glamorous images.

The extent of the problem

It's important to realise that for children and adults alike television, and other media to varying degrees, present two different sets of challenges. The first is that it's a passive, sedentary activity which can affect metabolism, mood, sleep and health. In short, extended television use – irrespective of what we watch – is detrimental. The second set of problems relates to what we watch – to the content. So this is about social comparison, commercialisation, materialism, violence and sexualisation. If you put both types of problems together you can see how negative television can be for everyone. Throw in the fact that television viewing undermines community and relationships and can be addictive and you can see how the media can negatively affect people's lives and health.

Given what we've seen in this chapter, it's hardly surprising that since the 1950s and the advent of television and the growth of the media we have witnessed unprecedented increases in consumption, personal debt, divorce, depression, anxiety and loneliness. It's hardly surprising that people increasingly feel that community life has weakened and that we are living in a society which is becoming more amoral. It's also easy to see why Western society should become dominated by the issue of self-esteem, given how people's sense of themselves can easily erode in consumer society. Of course, other social, cultural and economic developments have played their part in all these deleterious developments, but for the reasons outlined above, the media's impact appears to be substantial.

Given the copious health problems and social costs why is

there not more information and discussion about the effects of TV and at least some encouragement to cut down or switch off? The media play an enormous role in political life and media companies are not just very wealthy but, as we know from recent events, hugely powerful. So it's not in politicians' interests to challenge them. They may also think that the message should not come from government as it would look like unnecessary interference.

It's certainly the case that switching on the television, going online or picking up a magazine are voluntary activities. There is no element of coercion. 'Big Brother' is not ordering people to switch on. So people are likely to think that viewing and other media habits are their free choice and it's no-one's business what they do in their own homes.

Then there's what psychologists call 'cognitive dissonance': if I find out that I'm doing something which may not be good, rather than confront the problem, my own inadequacies or the fact that I need to change my ways, I'm more likely to deny the difficulty. This may be why people often accept that television viewing or advertising can be negative for others but think that they are personally immune.

The message that people need to hear is not that they, or their children, should never watch television – this is unrealistic and unnecessary. But we should all encourage parents to restrict youngsters' viewing times and what they watch. Adults also need to realise that, for their own well-being, they should be much more selective in what they watch on television. This will be challenging at first but will become more healthy and satisfying. To paraphrase Marx, viewers of the world unite you have nothing to lose but your remotes.

CHAPTER FIVE

Winners and losers

We live in a profoundly unequal society. More than almost any developed nation ours is a country in which your parentage dictates your progress. Those who are born poor are more likely to stay poor and those who inherit privilege are more likely to pass on privilege in England than in any comparable country. For those of us who believe in social justice this stratification and segregation are morally indefensible.

These words were not uttered by a leftie radical but by Michael Gove, the Conservative MP, who is currently Education Secretary in the UK Coalition government. And he's right. A report published by the OECD (2011) on income inequality across rich nations reported that it has risen faster in the UK, since the mid-1970s, than in any other nation. The study found that the gap between rich and poor had grown even in countries like Denmark and Sweden, which are generally fairer, but Britain's inequality is particularly pronounced. Those in the top 10 per cent of incomes in the UK earned 12 times more than the bottom 10 per cent; this is significantly higher than it was in 1985 when the ratio was 8 to 1.

When it comes to social mobility, the data confirm that there was some improvement in the 1950s and 60s but that this trend faltered and evaporated after the 1970s. OECD figures show that if we take what a person's father earned, and what they earn, as an indicator of mobility, the UK is the least mobile country in the developed world. The Sutton Trust reports that those born in 1958 were more likely to earn more than their parents than those born in 1970. For every one person from the poorest fifth of society going to university there are four from the top one fifth of society. People from wealthy backgrounds are also more likely to hold on to their wealth than they were in the mid twentieth century.

The barriers to social mobility can be see in the following figures: only 7 per cent of the UK's population goes to private schools yet 51 per cent of the top doctors, 70 per cent of judges, 54 per cent of FTSE 100 chief executives and 45 per cent of top civil servants attended private schools. As for top journalists, 54 per cent were educated privately and 45 per cent went to Oxbridge. Even a growing number of rock bands are now drawn from public schools, a phenomenon dubbed 'posh rock'.

When it comes to politicians, 35 per cent of MPs and 67 per cent of the current Westminster cabinet went to fee paying schools, including the Prime Minister and Chancellor who are old Etonians. In May 2010 when Cameron appointed his first Cabinet, 23 out of 29 were millionaires. Again this has not always been the case. From 1964 until Fettes-educated Tony Blair moved into Number Ten in 1997, Britain had a succession of state educated prime ministers.

The USA's story is very similar. Americans are relaxed about the idea of people making money and becoming rich but they want everyone to have the same opportunities to advance. The country once boasted high levels of social mobility but no longer. Recent research shows that intergenerational economic mobility rose in the USA from 1950 to 1980 and then declined significantly. America has also witnessed a huge and widening gap between the rich, who just keep getting richer, and the poor whose earnings keep falling. Professor Robert Putnam argues that social class in the US has now become a huge, and largely unrecognised problem, and that this divide is much more important than race.

And what of Scotland? Scotland was a marginally fairer place in terms of income inequality than England but by 2010 this was no longer true. Social mobility in Scotland has generally followed the same pattern as the UK as a whole with some improvement until the 1970s and then a reversal. The National Union of Students published research (2012) which showed that St Andrews University only had 13 students from 'poorer' Scottish backgrounds. Edinburgh and Aberdeen universities' figures are also low. This is to be expected as Scotland has the largest educational attainment gap in the OECD. In short, there is a pronounced difference between the school achievements of the rich and poor in Scotland.

However there are some differences between Scotland and England. Scotland has only 4.3 per cent of its population educated at public schools – lower than England's. However the percentage who attend fee paying schools in Edinburgh is similar to London's figures. The most noticeable difference between Scotland and England in terms of social mobility and inequality is the current generation of politicians. Alex Salmond went to a state school as did most of his cabinet and there are few, if any, millionaires in their ranks.

From the mid-1970s in the USA and the 90s in Europe research showed that people were becoming much more 'aspirational'. Various surveys also showed that people were increasingly looking to jobs as a major source of life satisfaction.

The expansion of university education which began in the 1960s played its part in this. Schools started to pressurise their pupils to do well academically so that they could go on to higher education and well-paid careers. Fee-paying and grammar schools had always performed this role but with the growth of universities, the rise of service sector jobs, the decline of traditional industries, and the pressure from central government and league tables, schools started to exhort their pupils to raise their aspirations. 'Equal opportunities' also contributed to this rise. Feminism which had once been about changing the world, ultimately became about women entering jobs previously occupied by men. Women are now less interested in marriage and children and want a career with prospects. Black people too have been encouraged to aspire for a better life and to see careers as the best route.

However, what's evident for women and black people is that there's a veneer of equality; the predominant notion is that there are no barriers to minorities getting on when in fact there is still 'institutional racism' in organisations like the police. Gender equality in the UK is also patchy with few women at the top of organisations. Despite this the former CEO of Marks & Spencer told women: 'You've got real democracy and there really are no glass ceilings, despite the fact that some of you moan about it all the time. Women can get to the top of any single job that they want to in the UK.' M&S cater mainly for women consumers and yet they do not have a female CEO and only 5 of 14 board members are women. The same is also true of its management committee. One of the reasons why barriers remain is that white men tend to appoint in their own image. Also, since most senior jobs in the UK, unlike Scandinavia, do not allow for flexible working then women who want to combine a career with motherhood find promotion extremely difficult.

The downside of an aspirational culture

Undoubtedly some people have led more interesting lives as a result of the new aspirational culture. However, as Oliver James documents, these developments may have had profoundly negative consequences for our well-being and our mental health. James, a clinical psychologist, tells us that to maintain a positive sense of self it's important that we find ways to 'discount' either our own shortcomings or other people's success. Thus if I meet a woman who is a powerful chief executive, I could discount her success relative to my own by telling myself she has got on because she went to a fee-paying school which prepared her much better for leadership than did my comprehensive education. James argues that people who are prone to depression are much more likely to engage in upward social comparison and don't use a process of discounting. So it's hardly surprising that they continually feel they are a failure in life as they will always encounter people who are much more successful than they are.

So one of the problems with the aspirational culture we now inhabit is that people who would have previously compared themselves with similar others (and not those higher in the social hierarchy) are now encouraged to use different benchmarks for their performance. For example, working women don't compare themselves with women of the past and think they are doing well. Instead they compare themselves with men who are much more likely to get on at work as a result of male networks, the inherent male bias which operates in many organisations and the fact that they are unlikely to be held back by parental responsibilities. Black people do the same, comparing themselves to successful white people. But as James points out this type of social comparison is a 'double-edged sword'. It encourages people to think they can achieve and raises aspirations (all to the good) but, given the in-built biases in the system (class, sexism and racism), then it's bound to fuel frustration and dissatisfaction.

Given these barriers people are, at best, confused if they are unable to make the progress they desire. At worst, they can feel resentful or begin to blame themselves for their inability to get on. James writes: 'If more of us are making upward social comparisons which we feel entitled to achieve but have virtually no likelihood of actually doing so, no wonder that more of us are feeling depressed because we are left feeling like helpless losers.' All of this is on top of the damaging social comparisons encouraged by television, outlined in the last chapter.

Our society's continual attempt to raise aspirations for money and success also encourages people to look to work as a source of fulfillment in life when it's unlikely to provide it. The problem here is not simply the in-built biases we have already discussed but the inescapable fact that there are restricted opportunities for advancement. Everyone can't be a leader, manager or top professional. By definition these posts are limited. For every one person who gets on there are countless more who are bound to miss out. As the Australian psychologist Gavin Hamilton points out 'In a society of winners and losers, most people lose.'

Having a job is of fundamental importance to people's well-being and unemployment can undermine people's physical and mental health. Nonetheless, as many organisations' staff surveys testify, for many people work is not that intrinsically satisfying. Indeed a major study by Robert Taylor called 'Britain's World of Work – Myths and Realities' based on a large-scale, in-depth survey carried out in 2000 found that there had been a significant decline in people's attitude to work since a similar study in 1992. They found that just as in the earlier study 'class' was of 'crucial importance' to the world of work' and that 'employee's satisfaction since 1992 had declined in every facet of their job.' Long working hours were a real source of disgruntlement particularly for 'highly educated males'.

Bronnie Ware, who worked for years nursing the dying, reports that one of the most common regrets is having 'worked too hard'. This was true, she says of all the men she nursed, as they often invested so much of their time in work that they had to forego the opportunity to see their children grow up, or spend time with their families. It was also true of the women who had worked. It's interesting that as women's lives have changed and they have either foregone having children to concentrate on work, or combined children with a job, that women's happiness has, on average, gone down, not up. In short, is the aspirational culture in which we live encouraging us all to overvalue careers?

Disrespect
Richard Sennett is an American sociologist who has devoted much of his life to issues of 'respect'. One of his earlier books is called *The Hidden Injuries of Class* (1972) and it analyses the lives of working class men – the types of men who regularly

feature in Bruce Springsteen's songs. The book describes how these men have been 'injured', 'humbled' and 'wounded' by class. They have grown up in an individualistic, though class bound society, which tells them that they are masters of their own destiny, yet so much is stacked against their success. Thus when they fail to succeed they have a crisis of self-respect and fear the judgement of others. This is why so many of them labour long hours so that they can acquire the money to give their children a good education and a way out of a life which they find so painful.

The idea that we need to feel respected by others, and that this is eroded in an unequal society, permeates an important book of our own day – *The Spirit Level* (2009) written by two epidemiologists, Richard Wilkinson and Kate Pickett. They provide evidence to support their argument that societies with low income inequality have better health, and less violence and social problems such as child abuse. They claim this is why Scandinavian countries like Denmark and Sweden have much better well-being and other social indicators than other rich, but more unequal countries, like America or the UK.

Wilkinson and Pickett argue that there are 'psycho-social' reasons why acute inequality in a society results in a whole range of social problems. They surmise that human beings' large brains, and speech, have evolved to allow us to interact socially with others and that we have great powers to empathise and identify with others' predicament and feelings. While we are capable of reinforcing our own status by excluding and discriminating against others, our psychological make-up means we experience real shame and embarrassment if others treat us as inferiors or if we even think we're being judged unequal in the others' eyes. If human beings (and many non-human primates) are forced into submission by another of higher rank then they will often turn and attack another lower in the pecking order. Primatologists call this the 'bicycling reaction' because 'animals show their back to the top while kicking towards the bottom'. Here's an account of how this reaction shows itself in baboons:

> Such third-party displaced aggression accounts for a huge percentage of baboon violence. A middle ranking male gets trounced in a fight, turns and chases a subadult male, who lunges at an adult female, who bites a juvenile, who slaps an infant.

This passage describes perfectly the world we now inhabit. Of course, past inequality has always been a driver for nastiness – sectarianism, racism, homophobia, the subordination of women, domestic violence, the treatment of children, animal cruelty, gang culture and so much more. Nowadays, we have political correctness and laws to advance equal rights and protect individuals from prejudice and hate, yet as inequality has risen steeply in the past few decades, the bicycling reaction is more evident in everyday life. For example, bullying is rife in our schools and workplaces and the reality TV shows which fill the schedules are based not only on judgement and voting people off, but also routine humiliation. 'You are the weakest link, goodbye' seems positively tame in comparison with today's genre of programmes which set people up to be mocked and disrespected. Susan Boyle is a beautiful singer and has won herself fame and fortune but when she first appeared on the *X-factor* stage she was insulted by the judges for her appearance and demeanour and jeered at by the audience. Look at pop videos and you'll see how often the story line revolves round humiliation and arrogance.

The unequal effects of materialism

In *The Wealth of Nations* (1776) Adam Smith explains that economic growth is particularly beneficial for the poor. Interestingly he does not portray the benefits simply in conventional economic terms – food and shelter, for example – he wants the poor to live without 'shame'. Indeed Smith passionately believes that human beings are social creatures who need the respect of others. This is why he argues that a poor man needs to own certain items of dress:

> A linen shirt, for example, is, strictly speaking, not necessary for life. The Greeks and Romans lived, I suppose, very comfortably, though they had no linen. But in the present times, through the greater part of Europe, a creditable day-labourer would be ashamed to appear in public without a linen shirt, the want of which would be supposed to denote that disgraceful degree of poverty, which, it is presumed, nobody can well fall into without extreme bad conduct.

In 2012 Dr Sandra Carlisle conducted focus groups with people from communities in areas of deprivation in Glasgow, Manchester and Liverpool. She was particularly struck by the strength of people's materialist values. For example, some women living on a very limited income appeared driven to spend money on 'personal display' (their appearance and visible possessions) with money for family food being squeezed. The point is that fashionable hair, a spray tan, and the latest gear were for them what a linen shirt was to a day labourer in Adam Smith's day. They also spent considerable sums of money on babies and would not consider using hand-me-downs or buying second-hand. Dr Kathy Hamilton from Strathclyde University conducted research into 30 low income families and found that they were drawn to 'conspicuous consumption', particularly buying the right 'brands' as a way to offset the stigma of being poor. As she points out the unfortunate effect of this is to attract further stigma as those who are better off are then critical of the way they spend their limited money.

Materialism, brands, deprivation and inequality feed off one another. As we saw in earlier chapters people who experienced poverty as children, or who feel financially insecure, tend to be more materialistic. Poor people are heavy TV viewers, soaking up television for five or six hours a day, often because they can't afford bus fares or the money to do other things with their time. Since people on the lowest incomes favour commercial television this means that they're much more exposed to adverts. So in our consumerist age what people think they need to live without feeling 'ashamed' is bound to rise dramatically – not just items of dress, but a well-equipped house with several good TVs, and the latest mobile phones. And to acquire these things people often get into considerable debt.

Since so much about our materialist culture is about buying things for status and not for their intrinsic value, the biggest casualties are poor people: spending money on goods to convey status and then scrimping on food, outings, or holidays does not make a positive contribution to well-being. Just as Tim Kasser's research shows, the obsessive focus on consumer goods and appearance takes people away from the things that really do contribute to a good life such as relationships, friendships and community involvement.

Phil Hanlon and Sandra Carlisle went on 'learning journeys' in Scotland and report some of their findings in the first book in this series – *AfterNow* (2012). They found that everywhere they went people were troubled by individualism and materialism. One of the members of the prisoners' group they spoke to made a particularly apposite observation:

> People live in their own bubble, getting in their own car to drive to work, staying in their own home. Community spirit has gone and this compounds the issue. We're all in debt. You're stressed, you go to work, you go home. You sit in front of the TV. There's no family dinner, no time to talk problems through, sort things out. You're just working to afford that TV. There's no time for your children when you come home at night. No time to talk.

Materialism also has negative effects on the better-off but as they have more money to spend, buying consumer goods does not necessarily restrict their access to culture, hobbies and the outdoors. Having money eliminates the stress of poverty and can take the pressure off relationships. It is also easier for those with money, education and secure employment to expand their psychological resources and personal skills and purchase support. So while the poor experience the full whack of materialism's negative effects the better-off are able to use their personal and financial resources to buffer them.

Sadly in the UK, our materialistic culture leads us to a myopic definition of deprivation. This comes to the fore in a study of child well-being in the UK, Spain and Sweden which we return to in the next chapter. The researchers tell us:

> For Spanish families, those who have no time with their children are 'the deprived' whilst in Sweden a family is unfortunate if they live in a neighbourhood 'where they are not free to roam outside.' But 'in the

UK inequality is firmly related to the amount of money (and by extension consumer goods) that we have.

Of course, poverty and inequality are big issues in the UK – more so than in Spain and Sweden. But alongside issues of poverty and inequality we must openly acknowledge the negative effects of materialism. If we don't we simply perpetuate the myth that to lead a good life we all need money for hair extensions, plasma televisions, branded trainers and the latest baby gear.

From gewgaws to hauling

Finally, let's hear once more from Adam Smith whose work is often used to justify ruthless economic expansion but who actually had very little time for the rich. In *The Wealth of Nations* he writes:

> When a man of fortune spends his revenue chiefly in hospitality, he shares the greater part of it with his friends and companions; but when he employs it in purchasing such durable commodities, he often spends the whole on his own person, and gives nothing to any body without an equivalent. The latter species of expense, therefore, especially when directed towards frivolous objects, the little ornaments of dress and furniture, jewels, trinkets, gewgaws, frequently indicates, not only a trifling but a base and selfish disposition.

Given his attitude to spending what would Smith make of the world we now inhabit? – a world in which we actively rear our children to focus on the trifling things in life and to cultivate 'a base and selfish disposition'.

These values are strikingly evident in a new internet phenomenon called 'hauling'. This basically involves girls sitting in their bedrooms in front of a camera as they hold up all the items they've bought at the shops and giving a commentary on them ('neat' and 'cute' get used a lot). They then put the video on youtube or facebook. There are literally thousands of videos available and some have more than a million hits.

If we take a generous view of hauling we could say that these girls are just being appreciative of their purchases. Perhaps they are trying to be genuinely helpful to their peers. Even if either of these explanations was credible, hauling would still rank as base and trifling in Smith's eyes. Have they not got something more worthwhile to do with their time such as helping out at home, taking exercise or pursuing their studies? A more cynical but no doubt realistic view of hauling is that it puts the haulier in the spotlight, makes them look 'hot' and leads others to feel envious. In making these videos these hauliers are showing no compassion for their contemporaries who don't have smart bedrooms, cameras, or money to go on a haul.

However, these girls are not personally responsible for the creation of our trifling, base and selfish culture – they are only being the savvy, good consumers they have been groomed to be since they could sit in front of a TV and watch adverts or programmes like Hannah Montana. They are completely in tune with the values and culture of consumer capitalism.

CHAPTER SIX

Families, kids and the new rock and roll

For thousands of years older people have worried that changes in society (reading, dancing, comics, cinema) were corrupting the young and undermining youth's morals and well-being. So should we be worried about materialism's effect on the younger generation? Emphatically yes, as we are now living in a world (at least in the UK) that is undermining children's mental and physical health. This is not just my contention. UNICEF undertook research into the well-being of children in twenty rich nations and those in the UK scored the lowest, just behind the USA. As much poorer countries had a higher placing, values, way of life or culture must play a part.

For the sake of brevity here are seven measures of child and youth well-being which have risen dramatically in the UK in the past few decades – depression, anxiety, obesity, self-harm, eating disorders, conduct problems and ADHD. Some of these have doubled or trebled since the 1950s. International data confirm that America has also seen significant rises in these types of problems while other European countries have not suffered to nearly the same extent.

The upward trend in the type of measures listed above indicate that all is not well with the way we are rearing our children in the UK and accords with the perceptions of those working with them. Older teachers continually report that they detect a loss of resilience in youngsters and rising mental health problems. Why?

Academics frequently cite research on samples of fifteen year olds from the west of Scotland collected in 1987 and 2006 as it presents convincing evidence of a significant rise in psychological distress for this age group (particularly for girls) in the past twenty years. A later analysis of why this might be the case concluded that the following factors were particularly salient: 'arguments with parents'; worry about 'family relationships' (particularly for girls); and 'school disengagement'. This echoes another in-depth influential study on the rise of mental disorder in the young. Both studies make some reference to growing materialism and individualism but then mainly plump for school and family factors as pivotal. However, if we probe further we see that materialism is key to changes within families.

Anver Offer is an Oxford professor and author of *The Challenge of Affluence* (2006). He's an economic historian so it's interesting that he spends considerable time writing about love, commitment and child-rearing. Drawing on a wide variety of sources he asserts: 'Affluence, marital breakdown and mental disorder have risen together since the 1970s.' This picks up on one strand of argument presented in the last chapter. Namely, that since the 1970s rising materialism has encouraged people to look beyond committed relationships and child-rearing for satisfaction in life and become more interested in self-expression and careers. Consequently marriage rates have fallen as has family size. Women's work commitments mean that they tend to spend less time with their children and professional fathers see their children less as a result of working patterns and commuting. Also, parental unions are much less stable as a result of higher levels of divorce and the instability of cohabitation. Offer summarises the research which shows that children with divorced parents are likely to suffer in life. Children of single-parents also tend to have much worse outcomes than those from two parent families. He points out that this is not inevitable – some survive and thrive – but that children whose parents divorce or who only have one parent are more vulnerable than those who live with both. Ever the economist, he writes: 'People seeking the best for themselves, in conditions where commitment was insecure, may have been shifting a cost into the future, in this case, onto their own children.'

Offer, however, does not seek to blame individuals. He admirably sets out how factors such as the media's commodification of sexuality, the continual promise of individual fulfillment and happiness via purchases or individual success, rising inequality and the pressures of modern life have altered the balance between men and women and undermined family life. This takes its toll on our intimate relationships and our children:

> In a turbulent, challenging, competitive environment
> . . . the quest for private self-actualisation, held out by
> the market, may have been self-defeating. Often,
> however, it was the only choice available. The
> withdrawal from commitment signalled the loss of
> security and attachment. It became a cycle in which
> anxiously attached parents transmitted their
> alienation to their children through the medium of

family discord. The children then sought solace for
psychic distress in materialism (or even drugs), and
their frustration eventually infected their own
parental priorities and capacity for attachment.
Driven by materialism, the cycle of discontent was
transmitted from one generation to another even as
affluence increased, to form an expanding patch of
misery on the pond of abundance.

As Offer himself admits many adults have led much more
interesting and stimulating lives as a result of this turning
away from the family and child-rearing. But nonetheless he
forces us to consider the price tag: a loss of mental well-being
for young people and generations yet to come. As happiness
and satisfaction have not increased overall in the UK and the
USA as a result of rising aspirations, self-expression and
supposedly fulfilling careers, then it's even more tragic that
we have collectively bought into this aspirational fantasy with
all its other costs.

The psychotherapist Sue Gerhardt agrees that the neglect
of children's basic emotional needs, particularly in the first
two years of life, is driving mental ill health and materialism;
that people's insecure attachments or inadequate emotional
development lead them to look to consumption for satisfaction rather than to relationships. Gerhardt worries that
women's working lives often depend on unsatisfactory day-
care for their young children but she is much more relaxed
about divorce and family structure.

In both Offer's and Gerhardt's work there is an emphasis
on relationships, particularly the bond between parent and
child and they provide a helpful link between the research
which says that children's deteriorating well-being is linked
to changes in family life and the increasing materialism of

our culture. This deterioration results from the simple fact that materialism plays down the importance of relationships and connections for individuals' satisfaction and well-being.

UNICEF

As we saw earlier, the UNICEF research into child well-being puts children in the UK at the bottom of the league table. This was a great indictment of the UK yet it was largely ignored by politicians. UNICEF commissioned some further research into the underlying causes. It was carried out by Dr Agnes Nairn and IPSOS Mori and published in 2011.

Nairn compares children and family life in the UK, Spain and Sweden, particularly focusing on inequality and materialism. Sweden was second in the 2007 UNICEF league table for child well-being and Spain, fifth in the list, has very high levels of subjective well-being despite inequality which is steep, though lower than the UK's figure.

One of the most striking findings is that children across the three countries were remarkably consistent in describing a 'good day'. This involved 'time with those they love (friends, family and even pets); creative or sporting activities; being outdoors and having fun.' It was 'people not things which made them happy.' Family time was also important and they did not see material possessions 'as essential to their well-being'. There was one exception to this: poor children in the UK were more likely to talk about purchases.

The main difference to emerge in this comparative research was parents' attitudes. The Swedes were child-centred with both parents involved and organising their work life round child care. They saw their primary role as raising responsible, independent citizens and they ensured children participated in household chores. In Spain mothers, supported by the extended family, mainly look after children. They loved spending time with children and being involved with them. Nairn writes that 'being a parent was natural in Spain and Sweden' and that 'time with the family is prioritised over work and other commitments'.

However, being a parent in the UK was 'strained'. The picture that emerges is of parents working long hours, often for low pay, and struggling to spend quality time with their children. Long hours were added to by long commutes and the working hours expected in higher paid jobs. UK parents also felt compelled to buy their children the latest brands or gadgets, fearing that their offspring would otherwise be bullied or left out. Nairn talks about a 'compulsive consumption cycle' which was absent from Spain and Sweden – 'consumer culture in the UK appeared in our research to be "disposable" with households full of broken and discarded toys and a compulsion to continually upgrade and buy new'. She adds, 'This stands in stark comparison with Sweden and Spain where toys and electronic gadgets were looked after, often mended when broken, and were cherished as long-term companions.' People sitting at home in different rooms watching TV was also a particularly UK phenomenon.

Nairn's research also highlighted another worrying trend:

> . . . the Spanish and Swedish parents we observed
> appeared to be more confident in their ability to
> draw and enforce boundaries, and more confident
> to say "no" to their children than was the case in
> the UK families. Negotiating the commercial world
> was distinctly more problematic in the UK and this
> was the case regardless of social circumstances.

One of the reasons why UK parents may give in and buy their children more is that the long working hours culture makes them particularly susceptible to what the advertising industry calls 'guilt money' or the 'I'm sorry syndrome'.

Commercialisation's grip on our children

> The conventional paradigm of childhood as a life stage that revolves around family and schools has had to change. It's the commercial world that dominates the time of today's children.

This is what Agnes Nairn and her co-author Ed Mayo write in their book *Consumer Kids: How Big Business is Grooming Our Children For Profit* (2009). But how on earth did we get here?

Advertising to children is not new. I can remember ads from my childhood including jingles and slogans. However, until the late 1980s the children's market was small and advertising's poor relation. Four factors resulted in change: a realisation that children had disposable income; more television programmes aimed at this age group; children viewing alone; and the decline of authoritarian parenting giving children influence on family spending. As the economist Juliet Schor says in *Born to Buy* (2004), 'By the 1990s the stage was set for a thorough revolution in youth marketing.'

Fast forward to our own time and the youth market is worth $188 trillion worldwide. In the UK spending on 5-16 year olds was £110 billion in 2009 and it had doubled in only eight years. Here are a few of the techniques big companies use to encourage young people to buy:

1. Employing psychologists, anthropologists and

sociologists to understand what makes children tick and to work out how to devise compelling messages to make them buy. Every aspect of children's lives is dissected with the aim of influencing their desire to consume.

2. Promoting the idea that to be socially acceptable kids needed to be 'cool' – thus instead of cheap, functional toys, the emphasis is on 'exclusive' and 'expensive'. In Schor's words 'Living modestly means living like a loser.'

3. Using 'age compression'. Originally this meant pitching teenage trends to those under twelve. Now it means 'tweening' – bringing teenage products to those between childhood and teen which can mean children as young as six.

4. Using children to get their parents to buy things. This is known in the UK as 'pester power'. Advertisers involved in these techniques openly talk about 'manipulating' children to force their parents to buy. In the USA a lot of car advertising is aimed at children. Inevitably this means marketing products on the basis of symbolism rather than functionality.

5. 'Trans-toying' – making everything from toothbrushes and shoes to food into something to play with.

6. Formally recruiting children as young as eight as salespeople to sell to their network of friends.

7. Seeing children as your company's future market. This may mean razor companies with no products for children providing free internet games so that they can create future loyalty to the brand.

8. Collecting personal information for marketing purposes on children online which some experts argue is akin to 'stalking'.

9. Being prepared to market drinks and food full of sugar,

calories, saturated fat or salt as 'healthy' and using athletes to promote them.

This is not just an American phenomenon. Nairn and Mayo assert that companies operating in the UK are 'child catchers' who see children simply as a market to exploit for profit.

Marketeers use terms like 'tweens' to obscure the distasteful fact that they are targeting primary school children. Even the huge Disney corporation which likes to market itself as family friendly and a protector of childhood innocence is nothing more than a massive marketing machine and their aim is to continually increase 'market share'. They are at the epicentre of the corporate world's attempt to commodify every aspect of children's lives.

When I was young I went to see Disney films, had a Cinderella toy that danced with Prince Charming and a few Disney colouring books. None of this mattered. Throw in a few more films, DVDs and a few products and I've little doubt that none of this would have a negative effect. However, the Disney Princess range alone (worth $4 billion) has 26,000 items for sale. The corporation markets its products on every available platform accessed by children not just in the USA but globally. Disney and other large-scale companies targeting the children's market are doing so on such a huge scale that they are colonising children's minds. Education professor Lyn Mikel Brown argues:

> Playing princess is not the issue. The issue is 25,000 products. When one thing is so dominant, then it is no longer a choice: it's a mandate, cannibalising all other forms of play. There's the illusion of more choices out there for girls, but if you look around, you'll see their choices are steadily narrowing.

It's hardly surprising that one frustrated mother called her book on the topic *Cinderella Ate My Daughter* (2011).

We know that children in the UK are exposed to advertising and the commercial world for seven hours a day on average. They know they do not need purchases to 'have a good day' but in the absence of quality time spent with parents and friends in creative or outdoor pursuits they will resort to materialist demands. Why wouldn't they given that the pressures to buy are everywhere and buying is so linked to status and 'being cool'? Three out of five children in the UK admit to pestering their parents to get what they want and will get annoyed if they don't get their demands met. Some young girls readily admit to being 'shopaholics', expressing guilt and remorse at buying things of no consequence to them.

Resisting young people's demands, limiting screen time and encouraging them to eat well, go to bed early and take exercise often makes parents feel that they are engaged in a battle with their children. Indeed because controlling their children's lives has become so challenging many parents admit that they simply give into the pressure for fizzy drinks and junk food. Under the weight of huge commercial pressures, children's diet and resultant obesity has become a major issue but because it has been extensively studied and discussed I've omitted it in this short book.

Sadly business and advertising have deliberately engineered some of the aggro between parents and children as it suits their purposes for kids to feel they inhabit 'a secretkid world' which adults don't understand. Juliet Shor explains that the commercial world is redolent with what is called 'antiadultism'. She admits that there has always been some generational conflict (though interestingly this does not exist in traditional societies) but that this has been deliberately exaggerated by marketeers. Since the 1960s the commercial word has success-fully engineered a separate culture for teenagers, complete with their own styles, fashion and language, and promoted the idea of teenage rebellion. However, this approach has 'trickled down' to younger and younger children. This started in the USA with the cable network 'Nickelodeon' which also has a massive reach into children's worlds through the web, games and products. Its core philosophy is 'Kids Rule'. According to Shor, an 'antiauthoritarian us-versus-them' attitude pervades Nickelodeon and a growing number of products and games aimed at young people portraying parents as repressive, boring, and joyless. A study of 200 video game ads between 1989 and 1999 reported that a common theme was 'the rejection of home environments as boring suburban spaces.'

Media expert Professor Mark Crispin Miller nails what's happening when he says: '. . . there's often a kind of official and systematic rebelliousness that's reflected in media products pitched at kids. It's part of the official rock video worldview. It's part of the official advertising worldview that your parents are creeps, teachers are nerds and idiots, authority figures are laughable, nobody can really understand kids except the corporate sponsor.'

This philosophy also permeates programmes aimed at kids with cartoon characters or boys and girls 'with attitude' speaking rudely and disrespectfully to adults as well as each other. Even the wholesome Disney corporation has darkened some of their characters. Mickey Mouse features in a new video game and he's lost his clean-cut image and is meaner.

Perfectionism and sexualisation

Finally, are materialist values and constant media exposure more damaging for boys or girls? In *Affluenza* Oliver James argues that the main casualties of the virus are middle-class girls as their distress has particularly increased since the late 1980s. His explanation is that girls are more eager to please so they are most vulnerable to the huge pressures to achieve.

Two years ago I spoke to a large group of fee-paying school head teachers in the UK who told me that their girls had fantastic achievements not just academically but in the arts and sports, yet observing these girls close up, to use their terminology, was 'not a pretty sight'. According to them these girls increasingly lacked resilience and were perfectionists. This meant that they were unable to take risks or make mistakes. They were equally obsessed by their looks. One research study has shown that over a third of women at an Oxford University college had at some point in their lives suffered from an eating disorder and 10 per cent were currently suffering. That is much higher than in the population at large. Indeed Oliver James argues: 'Perfectionism, academic success and eating disorders very often go together.'

We must also remember that children and teenage girls are now continually confronted with sexual imagery. A year ago I sat in the hairdressers at the sink beside an eight year old girl and on the screen before us was a music video which was so sexually explicit that until recently it would have been considered porn. Exposing young children to sexual imagery and designing clothes and other products with a sexual feel has recently become an important issue. The American Psychological Association set up a Task Force on the Sexualisation of Girls and undertook an in-depth analysis. Its report (2007) asserts:

In study after study, findings have indicated that women more often than men are portrayed in a sexual manner (e.g. dressed in revealing clothing, with bodily postures or facial expressions that imply sexual readiness) and are objectified (e.g. used as a decorative object, or as body parts rather than a whole person). In addition, a narrow (and unrealistic) standard of physical beauty is heavily emphasised. These are the models of femininity presented for young girls to study and emulate.

These psychologists argue that research shows that such self-objectification can impair cognitive function and undermine concentration and that it's also linked to eating disorders, low mood, depression and low self-esteem. They also argue that this sexualised view of women affects boys' and men's attitudes and undermines intimate relationships between the sexes.

On the other hand, a report commissioned by the Scottish Parliament's Equal Opportunities Committee (2010) concluded 'there is fairly good evidence that sexual imagery has become more widely available within the culture as a whole, including in material that is targeted at, or frequently consumed by, children' but they also assert that 'the evidence about the *effects* of this – whether positive or negative – is limited and inconclusive.'

This report, with its caveats and criticisms of almost every piece of research undertaken, has been praised by some for its thoroughness and open-mindedness but reading it made me lose the will to live. As we're about to see, the problem of sexualisation is a lot more worrying than music videos or padded bras for eight-year-old girls.

Video games and cybersex

While girls' achievements have increased at every level, not just in the UK but internationally, boys' results have gone down. In 2011 the famous psychologist Philip Zimbardo gave a TED talk called 'The Demise of Guys'. He recounts the fact that internationally boys are underperforming educationally and have growing problems with social interaction and intimacy:

> What are the causes? Well, it's an unintended consequence. I think it's excessive internet use in general, excessive video gaming, excessive new access to pornography. The problem is these are arousal addictions. Drug addiction, you simply want more. Arousal addiction, you want different. . . by the time a boy's 21 he's played 10,000 hours of video games, most of that in isolation. And the porn industry is the fastest growing industry in America – worth $15 billion annually.
>
> So the effect, very quickly, is it's a new kind of arousal. Boys' brains are being digitally rewired in a totally new way for change, novelty, excitement and constant arousal. That means they're totally out of sync in traditional classes, which are analog, static, interactively passive. They are also totally out of sync in romantic relationships, which build gradually and subtly. So what's the solution? It's not my job. I'm here to alarm. It's your job to solve.

In a follow-up survey 20,000 (mainly male) respondents were asked 'what factors contribute to motivational problems in young men?' and 62 per cent of boys aged 13 to 17 chose 'Digital entertainment (i.e. video games, pornography)'.

The impact this is having on boys' educational attainment

is trifling in comparison with its other effects. Pornography is not just one of the fastest growing industries, it's one of the biggest scourges of our time. It's important to realise that what's involved is very different from traditional 'girlie' magazines or erotica. Two journalists who have studied the industry in the USA can hardly convey their despair at what's being sold. One, Robert Jensen, a journalism professor, entitled one of his articles 'Pornography is what the end of the world looks like' for the simple reason that pornography mainly features degradation and some degree of violence against women. Erotic literature is fantasy but DVDs and internet porn convey scenes which have happened in real life, to real people. Chris Hedges is a Pulitzer Prize winning journalist and he has written about the porn industry arguing that it's driven by 'new ways to humiliate and inflict cruelty on women' – often young girls. It's hardly surprising that the women involved often need medical procedures and many are on drugs and pain killers. Hedges, who was a war correspondent with *The New York Times*, says that many of the women are obviously suffering from Post Traumatic Stress Disorder.

Pornography is now widely available on the internet, DVDs and mobile phones. According to Hedges the largest users of internet porn in the US are boys between the ages of twelve and seventeen. This is no accident as the industry targets adolescents. One European director of a porn company boasted to Hedges that 'the age demographic has moved downwards, especially in the UK and Europe. . . porn is the new rock and roll.' In this worldview porn is 'cool' and those who object to it are prudes.

As internet porn becomes more and more available the

usage figures continue to rise. Currently it appears that at least 50 per cent of males from 16 to 29 use pornography to some extent and boys as young as 11 can be heavy users. Some estimate that young men who use porn will do so for as much as three hours a week. Some men working with young men in Scotland say that many boys are beginning to realise that they're hooked.

There is now considerable research evidence that pornography has a real effect on males' attitudes to females. One researcher, Dr Michael Flood, writes: 'Consumption of pornography is exacerbating some males' tolerance for sexual violence, intensifying their investments in narratives of female nymphomania and male sexual prowess and shifting their sexual practices and relations.' In other words, pornography is normalizing sexual practices that previous generations considered deviant and encouraging men to link sexual gratification with violence against women. It completely undermines the idea that sex is best coupled with intimacy and connection. The youngest users of porn are particularly vulnerable as they have little idea of what is considered normal sex. This is one of the reasons why young men are so susceptible to adverts for 'enlargement'.

One recent survey in the UK showed that 54 per cent of boys found porn 'inspiring'. In other words, they wanted to imitate it. So it's no surprise that a 2009 study carried out for the NSPCC of 13 to 17-year-olds showed that 'a third of teenage girls in a relationship suffer unwanted sexual acts and a quarter physical violence.' Penny Marshall, a UK journalist, recently spoke to young people in London. None of the girls complained of violence but they talked about 'sexual bullying' particularly being pressurised into acts which the boys had seen on internet porn.

Philip Zimbardo, however, thinks that more commonly extensive pornography use is undermining boys' interest in real-life girls. There is certainly a logic to this: given that so many young men lack social skills and confidence, why bother with real girls at all if you can find a sexual outlet through pornography?

I started this chapter talking about young people's growing problems with mental health and how this has resulted in part from weakening family life, a lack of love and fractured relationships between men and women. Add in pornography and the way it can affect young men's attitudes to girls and sex and we have a particularly noxious brew with huge implications for our species.

Interestingly, it is male biology itself which may weaken porn's increasing popularity. Gary Wilson, an American science teacher and expert on pornography's effects gave a TEDx talk in Glasgow on the topic on the same day that I gave one on materialism. He explained that male sexual arousal is intimately connected with novelty – and the internet is fantastic at delivering this. The user is only one click away from a newer (though often more sadistic and deviant) sexual scene. Over time this continual ratcheting up of sexual experience makes the heavy porn user very vulnerable to chemical changes in the brain (higher dopamine). As the porn user keeps needing to find new sources of stimulation, the reward circuitry in the brain ultimately becomes 'burned out' because it is overstimulated. In short, the heavy porn user can easily find it more difficult to be turned on. As the problem is in the brain, not the penis, drugs such as Viagra will not help. Over time porn 'kills the male's arousal response' and he can then suffer from erectile dysfunction – the opposite of what porn supposedly offers men.

Far fetched? Here's some corroborating research: The Italian Society of Andrology and Sexual Medicine surveyed 28,000 men and found that those who started using porn in their teens and used it regularly were 'desensitized' and found it difficult to have sex with a partner. They also reported that this could be reversed within a few months if males gave up their porn habits.

Gary Wilson's work is testimony to the fact that a growing number of men now recognise the problem: after a few weeks of our TEDx talks being available on the internet mine had attracted 800 viewers and Gary's had almost a quarter of a million hits. Of course not all of these viewers have been influenced by the message they heard. Nonetheless Gary says there's evidence from various internet discussion sites that there's mounting concern. Substantial numbers of men are now giving up porn (not because it abuses women) but because of its disastrous effects on their sexuality – not a victory for justice but one in the eye for the porn industry and a very welcome development.

CHAPTER SEVEN

Business rules

Tony Judt was a British historian who dictated his last book *Ill Fares the Land* (2010) to students while he was dying. Judt made this effort as he believed that his generation, who could remember a time when money and the market did not dominate our lives, had to defend the virtues of social democracy. His opening lines are particularly pertinent:

> Something is profoundly wrong with the way we live today. For thirty years we have made a virtue out of the pursuit of material self-interest: indeed this very pursuit now constitutes whatever remains of our sense of collective purpose. We know what things cost but have no idea of what they are worth.

Thus far we have looked at how growing materialism has taken its toll on individual well-being. Now let's look at how, as a society, we got here and if anyone, other than authors like Tony Judt, is challenging these ideas.

'Turbo-capitalism'
Judt argues that until 1970 politics was dominated by issues of equality and fairness. People from all parties and walks of life would have thought it 'unthinkable to contemplate

unravelling the social services, welfare provisions, state-funded cultural and educational resources... that people had come to take for granted.' In short, the emphasis in politics was more about public good than private gain. This changed in the early 1980s with the emergence of 'market triumphalism' – an era when Ronald Reagan and Margaret Thatcher, in the words of the philosopher Michael Sandel, 'proclaimed their conviction that markets, not government, held the key to prosperity and freedom.' Bill Clinton, Tony Blair and ultimately Gordon Brown endorsed this philosophy believing that 'markets are the primary means for achieving the public good'.

In the UK Margaret Thatcher and successive governments sold off public assets in a great wave of privatisation. On both sides of the Atlantic greed was not just encouraged but held to be beneficial for both individuals and society. Capitalism can take various forms and, according to Edward Luttwak, the USA and the UK have 'turbo-capitalism' which gets its charge from privatisation, financial deregulation, low taxes on the rich, poor wage rates for workers and deregulation of the labour market. The proponents of this version of capitalism echoed Adam Smith in arguing that individuals pursuing their own economic self-interest kept government in its place. They also argued that everyone would benefit from economic expansion as 'a rising tide lifts all boats'. But as we have already seen, this has not happened as the massive expansion of the economy has made the rich much richer, widened inequalities and curtailed social mobility.

Michael Sandel argues convincingly that we should make a distinction between a market economy and a market society. The first is simply a way of organising production and distribution. Businesses make things and consumers decide if they want to buy. This can be an effective system which saves us from the problems of centralised planning and the production of goods which people don't want. Competition can also ensure that prices are low and standards high.

Sandel argues that if this market philosophy is not bounded by notions of right and wrong and penetrates the political and social world then we have a significant problem:

> Part of the appeal of markets is that they don't pass judgment on the preferences they satisfy. They don't ask whether some ways of valuing goods are higher, or worthier, than others. If someone is willing to pay for sex or a kidney, and a consenting adult is willing to sell, the only question the economist asks is "How much?" Markets don't wag fingers. They don't discriminate between admirable preferences and base ones. Each party to a deal decides for himself or herself what value to place on the things being exchanged.

> 'This non-judgemental stance towards values lies at the heart of market reasoning and explains much of its appeal. But our reluctance to engage in moral and spiritual argument, together with our embrace of markets, has exacted a heavy price: it has drained public discourse of moral and civic energy, and contributed to the technocratic, managerial politics that afflicts many societies today.

Through the course of this book we have seen the type of problem Sandel highlights. If you think that the consumer is king and markets free to do what they like then what's wrong with companies colonising young people's minds, lying about the health benefits of processed food or manipulating children to pester their parents to buy?

In the prevailing climate the winners are those peddling their own or their companies' self-serving agendas as nothing encourages them to think beyond their immediate self-interest or ask questions about the impact on others or the wider society. No wonder there has been a spate of research and books showing, for example, that if corporations were individuals they would be labelled psychopaths and that many leaders of corporations score high on narcissism.

The collapse of the gold standard in 1971 and the subsequent increase of footloose capital meant that many businesses became driven solely by profit. Investors – frequently foreign – increasingly wanted short-term results and they were largely indifferent to what the organisation was about. Money, and shareholder value, not the product, the employees or the wider community, are now all that matters in many corporations. Indeed Milton Friedman, Margaret Thatcher's hero, once said, 'The social responsibility of business is to increase its profits.' In the 1990s various progressives pinned their hopes on Corporate Social Responsibility to allay business's negative effects. Most now see it as little more than window-dressing.

Politics and the public sector

The type of economic changes required to 'turbo' charge capitalism were supported in part by cultural changes such as rising individualism and the emphasis on personal freedom. To understand the changes ushered in by the counterculture, advertisers devised 'market segmentation' and ultimately 'niche marketing'. In this expanded market of never ending desire to express yourself and be 'cool', business boomed.

American politicians were quick to use some of these new

marketing techniques and UK politicians, of both parties, soon followed. Peter Oborne in *The Triumph of the Political Class* (2007) explains how the new 'preferred method of communication involved marketing techniques drawn from the modern advertising industry.' Thus we entered a political era of 'focus groups' and spin doctors. According to Oborne:

> The political parties no longer took their ideas and beliefs from the aspirations of their membership, which had in any case largely disappeared. Nor did they refer back to their own underlying philosophies and beliefs. Instead they set policies only after remorselessly testing them on target voters in the key swing seats. Because all parties tried out their programmes on the same categories, their policies ended up being virtually identical. . .

Politics once involved political parties with different programmes and competing views on what would make society better. Now politics is about political leaders, appealing directly to electors on the basis of what would be good for them and their families' 'aspirations'. In short, politics has been individualised and voters are consumers, not citizens – consumers who get various perks in return for paying their taxes. Ironically this approach has done nothing for politics.

There are many reasons why there has been growing disenchantment with politics but the idea that politicians are 'all the same', not to be trusted and only interested in power certainly contribute to the widespread cynicism and apathy.

But can we blame politicians for simply trying to give voters what they want? This sounds defensible but the electorate are not deciding what they want on the basis of genuine free choice; as we have seen throughout this book we are now all embedded in a culture which at every turn reinforces the importance of buying, getting on, keeping up with the Joneses, being better than the Joneses, and looking after ourselves. If politicians of the left as well as right are simply going to accept that consumerism and individual financial success are what life is about then no wonder materialist values now completely dominate our society: there are no contrary messages. As we shall see, many people are looking for different values and they're not hearing them from mainstream politicians.

The encroachment of business into every area of life
These values are not just coming from the media, business and politicians. Business ideology and methods dominate almost every area of life. Even Charles Moore, a right-wing columnist, objects, writing: 'Government now affects a business style. At meetings which are not, and should not be, commercial, modern Civil Service language insists on asking what is the 'business case' for a particular course of action.' He cites other examples such as the introduction of business titles into the civil service such as 'Managing Director' and public bodies pushing out 'pseudo-commercial hype' such as 'customer-facing'. In Scotland it's now common for people to talk about 'Scotland PLC'.

Policy has also been affected. The last Labour Government introduced an internal market into the NHS in England and Wales and the Cameron Government has now opened up large sections of the NHS to profit-making companies. The Scottish Government has not followed suit and we should welcome this but it has supported what some believe is the insertion of inappropriate ideas from business into Scotland's leading arts organisation. Columnist Joyce McMillan writes of recent changes at Creative Scotland:

> . . . its thinking is still hopelessly infected – 22 years
> after the lady's political demise – by a kind of
> undead Thatcherism, a half-baked, hollowed-out,
> public-sector version of market theory that reduces
> the language of creativity to a series of flat-footed
> business school slogans, and imposes a crude ethic
> of sado-competition – "this will make you sharper
> and more creative" – on areas of society where co-
> operation and mutual respect matter more.

Some think that the radical edge has already been taken off
the Edinburgh Fringe by commercial pressures and that only
those with spare cash can perform.

It is widely accepted that both north and south of the border
universities are increasingly run as businesses and use the
language of business in their everyday operations. In 2008
Professor Stephen Ball said of the whole sector: 'Higher
education is increasingly a global business, and public-sector
universities are now participating in that global business in
an increasingly businesslike manner. . . It is difficult to
determine what counts as a public university any more.' He
added, 'There is a tension between a commercial model of
higher education and forms of learning and knowledge that
don't have a commercial value.'

Everywhere we look these days there is an emphasis in the
public sector on 'choice' and 'personalisation'. Of course,
some choice is beneficial but more is not better. Indeed there
is a large body of evidence that the choices we have in life
can overwhelm, distract and lead us to ruminate on whether
we have made the right choice thereby undermining our life-
satisfaction and well-being. Nonetheless, the mantra that

choice is good is now widely accepted by public officials. Interestingly, American research shows that if you ask people if they had cancer would they like to choose their own treatment, 65 per cent say yes.If you ask people who have cancer the figure is only 12 per cent.

Materialist values are also having an impact on people's career choices. Those training doctors report a noticeable increase in the number of medical students who now say that they came into medicine 'for the money'. In recent years a number of scandals have revealed a huge compassion gap in modern nursing. There are a variety of reasons why nurses are 'too posh to wash' or too busy to feed patients, including staffing levels and the way the profession is trained and managed. Nonetheless those training nurses also say they see a rise in the number of students who are simply interested in a career and who don't see nursing as a vocation.

And what of education? Suffice to say, that it's widely accepted by educational researchers and child well-being experts that there's now so much more pressure on pupils to achieve that many feel stressed by it. In recent years governments (particularly in England) have been manoeuvring for increased centralised control as a way to raise standards of achievement. It's now commonplace in Western countries for politicians to see education not as a way to develop children for life but as one of the best ways to develop the economy and compete in a global world. The adoption of personalisation in education can give the impression that education is becoming more child-centred whereas it's consumer culture itself which has stimulated politicians' interest in giving children more choice. The ultimate purpose of personalisation is still to equip young people to be good economic agents. In short, materialism rules in the classroom as much as it does elsewhere in contemporary society.

Charities, the New Age and the church

Political life and much of what we think of as the public sector have now been commercialised and are using business tools and perspectives to view the world but what about the third sector?

There are many small charities in Scotland and the rest of the UK whose values are decidedly unmaterialistic and their operations are much more in tune with their values than the dictates of business. They are the last bastion of non-materialistic values. Sadly, the same cannot be said of the big charities and they themselves are increasingly aware of this.

In 2010 a number of large UK charities including WWF, Oxfam and Friends of the Earth published a report based on a lengthy piece of research and consultancy called 'Common Cause'. Tim Kasser, whose work permeates this book, was one of the main advisers. The report uses the term 'extrinsic' rather than materialist but it essentially identifies the same shift in society that we have focused on here. For simplicity we'll keep using 'materialism'.

The report is important as it is an open acknowledgement from this sector that the problems they address (world poverty and environmental challenges) are driven by self-centred materialist values – money, appearance and status. These big charities admit that there will not be sizeable inroads into these problems unless people undergo a values shift and become less focused on themselves and more concerned with what they call 'bigger-than-self' problems.

The fascinating aspect of the Common Cause report is the open admission that currently these big charities are doing little, if anything, to bring about this value shift. The reason is simple: in their communications and campaigns they use techniques devised by business, advertising and the media – one of the main drivers of the problems they are trying to address. In other words, as these big charities engage with the public for their good causes, up till now they have mainly reinforced materialist values rather than actively try to supplant them or encourage other ideas. For example, charities involved in environmental campaigning will sometimes use arguments some refer to as 'green cool' – be the first of your neighbours, friends to get the latest. . .

Here's one of my own examples of the use of mainstream marketing techniques by this sector. I gave money to a big charity's campaign to feed children in the third world. I was then plagued by a series of emails from them where the subject line read 'Carol, we think you are special'. The email then attempted to flatter me as a result of my financial donation: the same values of narcissistic individualism, which currently suffuse the media, but in this case allied to a good cause. 'Limited edition goats' were available on a charity website where people could invest in goods for the third world to give as presents. This was no doubt tongue in cheek but was probably lost on many shoppers and simply reinforces the market's grip on our lives.

If you ever attend a big charity function you will be aware that the values of celebrity culture are writ large: visible in the encouragement of over-the-top dressing, the rich display-ing their wealth in conspicuous bidding at auctions, and the word 'luxury' appearing on most raffle prizes. Charity women's lunches often revolve round fashion shows and Gucci handbags.

What I'm arguing may seem too 'hair shirt' and serious but consider this: altruism is vital for human survival and may be why we are rewarded for compassionate behaviour by pleasurable feelings. Research shows that doing good deeds activates the reward circuitry in the brain and makes us feel happy or good. Indeed research demonstrates that people often have more pleasurable feelings when they spend money on others than on themselves. Secondly, human beings are moral creatures. As Barry Schwartz argues: 'nothing motivates people to do the right thing other than the desire to do the right thing'. So when charities use instrumental, self-serving or narcissistic reasons in their advertising they are actually distracting people from these wider philanthropic goals.

The Common Cause work is extremely challenging as many of the big charities are awash with marketing graduates or people with business experience and they direct their organisations' interface with the public. Nonetheless they have not shied away from these important issues.

What about the part played by the personal development or New Age movement? Undoubtedly some of this focuses on matters relevant to what we've covered here – namely how people can live satisfying lives which 'do not cost the earth'. Some books or practices on eastern religious and spiritual beliefs, or offshoots such as mindfulness, encourage people to find satisfaction within and live in harmony with others and the environment. But much of the personal development world is obsessed with individual success and increasingly with money. For example, much of the material espousing 'the law of attraction' such as that multi-million dollar phenomenon 'The Secret' are little more than an encouragement for people to focus on how they can get rich quick. When it doesn't happen they are the ones to blame for not wanting it enough and attracting it in their lives. .

Finally, what about the church? Does it not give a much-needed counterweight to materialism? In the USA the Protestant ethic ultimately, to use the historian David Landes' terminology, 'degenerated into a set of maxims for material success and smug, smarmy sermons on the virtues of wealth.' The current era of 'turbo-capitalism' has seen the emergence of 'the prosperity gospel' where God wants you to be rich.

Matters are somewhat different in the UK. After a period of reflection I concluded that the only time people can regularly hear someone deliberately trying to counter materialist values is on Radio 4's *Thought for the Day* which is broadcast to a very small audience. The church has some staunch critics of materialism in their midst. The former Archbishop of Canterbury Rowan Williams, for example, has been an outspoken critic of the present economic system and materialism. The Assembly of the Church of Scotland famously took Mrs Thatcher to task for her speech praising the free market, often referred to as 'the sermon on the Mound'.

I have little doubt that people involved in many churches in Scotland will be sympathetic to the arguments advanced in this book but, up till now, they have not been vocal, or active enough to impede materialism's progress. Indeed, by not repeatedly voicing their concerns on this topic and obsessing over gender and sexuality their message has been irrelevant to people who have to grapple every day with materialism's negative effects on individuals and society.

And what of that other great religion – football? If I were male, or a sports fan, no doubt I would have filled this chapter with page after page on how sport has become big business and is now dominated by materialist values. But this is a small book and, particularly in the wake of the 2012 Olympics, much of this is self-evident. But it's worth acknowledging that football has been a particular casualty of rising materialism and commercialisation. Many clubs are now the playthings of millionaire businessmen; top footballers are celebrities who can negotiate multi-million pound contracts; and money regularly trumps principle, decency or fairness as the elaborate tax avoidance schemes testify. The fans pay hefty ticket prices yet hardly matter anymore. Scotland knows this story well as Rangers, one of its oldest clubs, has been a casualty. Columnist Kevin McKenna is right to point out that there's a real clash in culture between the fans' sense of financial rectitude and contemporary business realities:

> It is hard not to feel sympathy for the ordinary
> Rangers supporter. While very rich and garlanded men
> were creating this scandal, the rank and file have
> continued donating a significant portion of their
> incomes in the struggle to save the club. Not long
> after the list of creditors was published by the
> administrators, assorted supporters' groups began to
> organise special fundraising events. Soon some of the
> small businesses that were owed money by Rangers
> were visited by fans and asked to accept handfuls of
> notes by way of payment for services rendered.

As KcKenna points out the irony was that while the supp-orters were acting in this unselfish way the administrators and advisors were being paid handsomely.

CHAPTER EIGHT

A different kind of moral collapse

For five days in the summer of 2011 people rioted in the streets of London and other English cities. The riots started in Tottenham and quickly spread to 66 different areas. Much of the disorder involved 'aspirational looting' whereby rioters targeted shops selling expensive brands and desirable consumer goods. The Prime Minister, David Cameron, used the riots as an opportunity to continue his campaign to mend 'broken Britain' – a phrase originally used by *The Sun*. He gave a lengthy speech claiming that in parts of the country there was 'a slow motion moral collapse' citing as the causes 'irresponsibility, selfishness, behaving as if your choices have no consequences, children without fathers, schools without discipline, reward without effort, crime without punishment, rights without responsibilities, communities without control'. Britain's many 'troubled families' were to blame and so too were gangs, failing schools, the effect of political correctness on politicians, the action of some government departments, and the health and safety culture. In a speech of over 4,000 words he never uttered the word 'inequality' yet London, the epicentre of the riots, is the most unequal city in the West and inequality is a cause of many social problems.

Up to now we have mainly focused on how materialism

undermines individual well-being. In passing we have encountered various social problems but let's now turn our full attention to how materialism undermines morality and causes social, economic and ultimately environmental problems.

Blaming those with least power and influence

After the riots, the Prime Minister commissioned a panel of researchers to investigate their causes and to make recommendations to stop them happening again. It's a lengthy report which echoes many of the issues I've already presented. It rules out the argument that the riots involved gangs or wayward children saying that the rioters were young people from some of the UK's poorest areas. In a summary paragraph the report states: 'Time and time again the same themes came up: a lack of opportunities for young people; perceptions about poor parenting and a lack of shared values; an inability to prevent re-offending; concerns about brands and materialism; and finally issues relating to confidence in policing.'

The panel accepts that there's a problem with policing, public sector provision and institutional responses in some of the neighbourhoods involved but tacitly they lay the blame on parents and young people themselves. This is why so much of the report focuses on building young people's 'character' and 'resilience' and boosting self-esteem and aspirations. They accept that there's a problem with advertising and brands but simply call on the Advertising Standards Authority to make some changes such as running a 'new school education programme to raise resilience among children'.

I've little doubt that poor parenting is an increasing issue as is lack of self-control and resilience in growing numbers of young people. But if we want to understand 'broken

Britain' or a 'slow motion moral collapse' we have to look to the top. As the Chinese say: 'The fish rots from the head.'

Interestingly, the only acknowledgement in the riots report that attitudes in wider society may have contributed is in a section where the authors raise the need for 'responsible capitalism' and more Corporate Social Responsibility. The values and standards of behaviour displayed by politicians, bankers and the media are not even acknowledged. Even David Cameron devoted 64 words in his 4,000 word speech on 'broken Britain' to this theme: 'In the highest offices, the plushest boardrooms, the most influential jobs, we need to think about the example we are setting', he declared. 'Moral decline and bad behaviour is not limited to a few of the poorest parts of our society. In the banking crisis, with MPs' expenses, in the phone hacking scandal, we have seen some of the worst cases of greed, irresponsibility and entitlement.'

The rotting head

In many of the current books on increasing social fragment-ation and moral decline there's widespread acceptance that in the late nineteenth century and earlier part of the twentieth century there was a sensibility about fairness and morality in public life. Peter Oborne asserts that in the Victorian era, 'The governing class internalised the idea of public duty.' It then set about a range of reforms which rooted out bribery and corruption, ensured transparent recruitment, and set standards in public life. The changes were designed to ensure that people couldn't use public office for their own purposes. These values were at the core of political life and were expected in other areas such as boardrooms and professional bodies. Tony Judt argues that the tenor of political life has now changed: 'We no longer ask of a judicial ruling or a legislative act: Is it good? Is it fair? Is it just? Is it right? Will it help bring about a better society or a better world? Those used to be the political questions, even if they invited no easy answers.'

The dominant question current mainstream politicians seem to ask themselves is 'will it bring economic growth?' and 'will it get us elected or re-elected'? Materialism, not morality, rules in so many areas of life. For so many who hold power, it's self-interest, success and money which matter more than integrity, justice or equality.

You may think I'm overstating the case, yet the UK has recently been rocked by a series of high level scandals – MPs' expenses, phone hacking, fixing of the interbank rate, Libor, and tax evasion on a grand scale. 'Power, Corruption and Lies' was *The Guardian's* banner headline after the Leveson Inquiry into press standards took evidence from a senior Metropolitan Police figure. She revealed that *The Sun* had established a 'network of corrupted officials' and created 'a culture of illegal payments'.

Over the centuries, philosophers and theologians identified a range of virtues such as prudence and temperance. But because there are prudent murderers and courageous despots, many argued that it's *justice* which underpins every virtue. Justice is commonly defined with reference to two things: conformity to the law; and equality among individuals or a sense of proportionality. Adam Smith believed sympathy fundamental to human interaction and applauded 'beneficence' but he gave a much more important place to justice:

> Society may subsist without beneficence. . . Justice,
> on the contrary, is the main pillar that upholds the
> whole edifice. If it is removed, the great, the

> immense fabric of human society. . . must in a
> moment crumble into atoms.

Another philosopher advised the following test for justice:

> In any contract and exchange, put yourself in the
> other person's place. . . and see if, in his place, you
> would approve of his exchange or contract.

Few can look at growing pay differentials in the UK and find them just. An independent High Pay Commission published its findings in 2011. It reports that the disparity between what top executives and average workers earn has been building since the late 1970s but has 'ballooned' in recent years. The people who reap the benefits are not as in previous centuries, the landed gentry or entrepreneurs, but 'the working rich' – bankers and business leaders. Here are a few choice statistics from the report:

- The pay of top executives at a number of FTSE companies has risen by more than 4,000 per cent on average in the last 30 years. Many of these executives now have multi-million pound packages per year made up of salary, bonuses, shares, pensions, etc. Basic pay has risen considerably, not just bonuses.

- In 2010 alone executive pay rose by 49 per cent on average. This compares with an average of 2.7 per cent for employees in the same year.

- Between the mid 1970s and 2008 the general workforce share of GDP shrank by over 12 per cent.

Few people object to top managers receiving more pay than others. But when senior people get so much money they can't possibly spend it then all sense of fairness and proportion has been lost.

The Commissioners assert that the move to high pay started with the 1979 Thatcher Government which had a new attitude to top pay: it believed that linking executive pay to perform-ance would create a dynamic, entrepreneurial elite at the top of business. However, as the report points out, 'no reputable study' has linked executive pay with company performance and this has become increasingly obvious in recent years when executives have been awarded huge bonuses even though the company's performance has decreased.

It isn't only the private sector which pays bonuses: government workers and senior managers working in public sector industries, or arms length organisations, have been paid performance bonuses on top of high salaries, often for indifferent performance. In 2010, after the financial crisis, the government paid 1,050 senior civil servants annual bonuses ranging from £8,000 to £20,000.

The High Pay report rightly points out: 'Over the last thirty years we have lost touch with what fair pay is. Indeed it has been undermined by a process that simplified individual motivation to that of self-interest.' It's certainly ironic that for decades now psychological studies have shown that financial incentives motivate when people are carrying out physical or mundane factory work. However, for jobs that involve intellectual skills monetary rewards can undermine performance and motivation. Job satisfaction, recognition, opportunities for advancement and doing something mean-ingful which engenders pride, can be much more motivating than money. Sadly this research has played no part in the current debate about bonuses. Instead there's an unthinking acceptance that people are only motivated by money and we've lost all sense that people may work hard because they have a strong sense of duty or simply enjoy their jobs.

Those defending gigantic remuneration packages argue that high-paid leaders are uniquely talented and will be poached by other countries if they're not given what they want. However, there's no evidence that CEOs will, or can, move easily from one big company to another. It's not good for companies to pay excessively high salaries and bonuses to CEOs. Peter Drucker – the foremost management expert – argues: 'If the top executive in a company gets a salary several times as large as the salaries paid to Number two, Three or Four men, you can be pretty sure that the company is badly managed.' Malcolm Gladwell goes further arguing there's a 'talent myth': it's effective teams that usually underpin healthy organisational performance, not high-profile charismatic leaders who often score high on narcissism.

The debt problem

The other groups benefiting from significant wage increases over the years are accountants, doctors, lawyers, and senior local government officers and civil servants. They are now paid substantially more than they were thirty years ago. Those in lower paid jobs have, in relative terms, seen their earnings eroded. This is not only unfair but has also contributed enormously to our economic woes.

We're all living in a consumer society where we're constantly urged to spend. Indeed our sense of worth may depend on having a bigger house than we can afford, maintaining a certain lifestyle and buying the latest gear. So if we're not able to buy what we want, because our income is too low, then all we need do is borrow, take the biggest possible mortgage and use credit cards. In the past thirty years personal debt in the UK has skyrocketed: in 1980 the debt/income ratio was 45 per cent, in 2007 it was 157.4 per cent. At the end of May 2012 personal debt in the UK stood at £1.460 trillion– up on the previous year's figure. To put this in context, individuals owed almost as much as the entire UK produced during 2011. The daily value of plastic card transactions in the UK in March 2012 was £1.392 billion. Average household debt, excluding mortgages was £7,891 and including mortgages £55,514. The Office for Budget Responsibility predicts this debt mountain will grow and that UK personal debt will reach £2.0444 trillion in 2017. As most people's wages are not rising in line with inflation people are now saving less per month than a few years ago. A Co-operative Bank survey showed that 20 per cent of people in the UK have no savings. Those under 35 are three times more likely to have no savings than the over 55s.

A few years ago, in terms of personal debt, the UK was second highest in the international league table, below the USA. However, their figure has improved and the UK now has the highest level of personal indebtedness (as a proportion of GDP) of all developed economies. It has taken a lot of maxing out on credit cards ('because you're worth it') and mortgages to get us to that position. Recent data show that if we aggregate personal, company and state debt, the UK is the most indebted country in the world – much of this comes from our financial sector. UK government debt is also considerable: In June 2012 it stood at £1.04 trillion.

Some argue that one of the drivers for government debt in the UK in recent years has been our low wages. Half of all UK children living in powerty have at least one parent in work yet they earn too little to take them above the poverty line.

Indeed the chance that working famlies will fall into poverty continues to rise as a result of 'the falling wage share'. As the TUC points out, this means that 'government policies have had to work much harder than in the past to reduce the level of poverty, and to check the extent of final income inequality.' Income support for families (e.g. child benefit and working family tax credits) almost doubled between 1996 and 2006.

In short, the state has been subsidising low wages thus allowing companies to chalk up higher profits. Because 'the low wage economy means that those on benefits can often be little better off financially by moving into work' it has also intensified the poverty trap. As those on benefits have become less keen on taking jobs it then inevitably increases the notion that the poor are lazy and unworthy of support.

The UK has followed the USA in promoting 'turbo capitalism' and all this implies – deregulation, low wages, and steep inequality. Lots of research has shown that pronounced inequality translates into various health and social problems so the UK was bound to see mounting problems 'troubled families', teenage pregnancy, a rising tide of mental ill health and elderly people plagued by loneliness. The USA's political culture tolerates this as it holds individuals responsible for their own lives but the UK is a society which still cleaves to the idea of a welfare state. Public services and intervention and support for poorer families and those in trouble were all bound to grow. How were they to be funded?

As a result of market capitalism, rising individualism and consumer politics, governments have been keen to cut higher levels of income and inheritance tax and give tax breaks to business. Without this revenue UK governments have funded a significant proportion of public services through debt – in effect, shifting the burden on to upcoming generations. However, it was bailing out the banks which led UK government debt to soar. According to the IMF, the UK has put £1.2 trillion behind the financial sector – that's over £19,000 for every man, woman and child.

The financial crisis

The Thatcher government deregulated financial markets in 1986. 'The Big Bang', as it is often called, abolished the regulatory barriers which separated the activities of banks, merchant banks, traders and brokers. This helped the globalisation of financial markets with London as a major hub of free-wheeling speculation. Critics of the move said it would destabilise the economy by undermining traditional British industry and privileging the financial sector and they've been proven right. Financial deregulation was brought in by the Conservatives but enthusiastically supported by subsequent Labour governments. Indeed only a few months before the crisis Gordon Brown told financiers: 'This is an era that history will record as a new golden age for the City of London.'

The financial crisis was triggered in 2007 by anxiety about the repayment of sub-prime mortgages in the US and we subsequently witnessed a domino effect with British financial institutions going to the wall or needing large government bailouts. European banks also required injections of cash, thus triggering a sovereign-debt crisis in Ireland and Spain and threatening the Euro itself.

The financial crisis crystallises one of the main themes of this book namely that a love of money, and unbridled materialism, squeezes out integrity and justice. We cannot run a country on the basis of empty, debt-fuelled consumerism and an ethic of 'get rich quick'. So it is hardly surprising that the collapse of the financial sector included the following factors – the extensive use of debt as a way to compensate for low wages; the highly questionable, if not immoral, lending of money to people who were unlikely to be able to repay (e.g. sub-prime mortgages); and a deliberate masking and then passing on of bad debt to other institutions.

In the summer of 2012 matters worsened for the banks when it became evident that Barclays Bank and others had manipulated the internet bank lending rate, Libor, for their own purposes. In the words of Aditya Chakrabortty:

> So in a sequence of events reminiscent of the Wall Street crash of 1929, the same industry that brought you a financial crisis, a double-dip recession and the greatest economic misery in decades is now vomiting up scandal after scandal.

> Shot through these iniquities is a high-handed sense of being above the law. It's obvious in the blatancy with which Barclays went about rigging interest rates even at the height of the crisis while taxpayers were bailing it out with subsidies and guarantees.

> . . . this isn't just an everyday story of ordinary banking folk constantly hatching schemes to pervert markets, morality and the course of justice. . . in the Libor scandal and elsewhere, the real picture is of an industry allowed to run riot by their regulators and governments.

Radicals, particularly young people, have shown their anger about what's happened to the economy through the 'occupy' movement. The average citizen has not protested in the street but is nonetheless angry about the extensive bonus payments to executives even in failing and bailed-out banks. What many find unacceptable is that citizens are losing public services as a result of the government's austerity package, and many public servants will lose their jobs. Yet no banker has gone to jail and many continue to be rewarded handsomely.

And what of Scotland? Scottish institutions were part of the problem: two of the country's oldest banks would have collapsed if they had not been propped up by UK government money; Scottish MPs – most notably Gordon Brown and Alistair Darling were at the eye of the storm; and the evidence suggests that political leaders in Scotland, including Alex Salmond leader of the SNP, supported financial deregulation. The scandal of huge bonus payments following the injection of government money has continued to dog RBS.

The real losers – the environment and our grandchildren
In the past few years various economists have written books questioning the wisdom of making economic growth the centre of government policies. After all, there's no reason to believe that continued growth in a wealthy society will increase stocks of well-being: other measures may be more beneficial. But thanks to the financial crisis the economic growth agenda has become even more prominent as future economic growth will help pay off the huge burden of debt.

But continually attempting to boost economic growth is a short-sighted strategy since the real casualty will be the environment and thereby the long term well-being of our children and grandchildren. Indeed mainstream politicians are now so focused on trying to get us back to normal that they're ignoring or playing down environmental challenges. And let's be clear here that 'normal' means continuing to focus on conventional materialist values including high levels of consumption – the root of so many of our problems.

In recent years green issues have been associated with 'global warming'. But in the face of cold winters and a few vocal critics who argue that climate change is not man-made, the public remain unconvinced. The abnormal weather patterns around the world and the rising tide of floods may change people's minds as they start to see the effects of climate change happening before their eyes. But focusing on the overuse of resources may be a more productive strategy: climate science is complex but people understand clearly that we cannot keep using resources in a finite world. Ordinary people also understand that our way of life damages habitats, destroys bio-diversity and generates so much waste that it's damaging the planet. In short, people easily understand that consumption has huge environmental costs.

Part of the problem is knowing what we can do as individuals. In the attempt to get people to believe that we can all make a difference we are encouraged to focus on making small changes such as turning off lights, using our own shopping bags, or recycling. But even if we all made these small changes it would hardly dent the problem.

For us to tackle environmental problems we need individuals to freely choose to make changes in their lives but we also need to know that we are tackling the problem collectively. For this to happen we need a shift in values and that means countering the materialism which has taken over so much of our lives.

CHAPTER NINE
Hope

In 2010 during the general election campaign I received an unexpected telephone call from Radio 4 asking me if I wanted to participate in an informal, on-air lunchtime discussion on the campaign with Martha Kearney. The other two guests were Professor Karol Sikora, the famous cancer specialist and critic of the NHS and Patrick Hennessy, a former officer in the Grenadier Guards turned author. At first glance we appeared to have different views thus guaranteeing a lively discussion. But even before we went on air we realised that we had very similar views: we all found the general election campaign deeply disappointing as leaders from all three parties simply wanted to get the country back to 'business as usual' – growth and spending. As electors we were looking for new values and more openness and honesty that we were never going back to a world that was increasingly dysfunctional.

We were not alone. Following the May election an American pollster and political strategist, Stanley Greenberg, conducted a post-election poll on a cross-section of UK voters. It showed that neither of the main parties' agendas convinced voters: Labour did not manage to persuade its core electors from working-class areas that it would improve their lives and the

Conservatives did not get people to support policies in favour of low tax or smaller government. Labour voters cited as their main reason to support the party its defence of the NHS and schools and Conservative electors were most likely to say that they didn't want Gordon Brown to continue as Prime Minister and thought it 'time for a change'. Many Liberal Democrat voters cited electoral reform as a reason for supporting the party. Across all those polled (including Conservative voters) there was strong support for measures to tackle inequality (66 per cent); for 'more government over markets' (71 per cent); and more financial regulation (56 per cent).

Stanley Greenberg said of their findings: 'People were looking for a vision, a direction for the country and a new set of values. They were looking for strategies for Britain to be successful and new definitions of the word success and they didn't see any of it.'

Everywhere I go I have discussions with people on the themes raised in this book and I'm struck by the common concern and consensus. Yes, most of them are in Scotland but I've also given talks in England and various European countries.

There is also 'hard' evidence to support the claim that there is much more support for a major values shift than you would think if you confined yourself to listening to politicians' speeches. Let's first start with the USA.

In the belly of the beast
In January 1995 an extensive research programme was launched in America involving focus groups in different areas of the country and a national public opinion survey. Its results were published in a report called 'Yearning for Balance: Views

of Americans on Consumption, Materialism and the Environment'. What emerges strongly is that Americans believe that their country's priorities are wrong and that they are increasingly driven by the wrong values. 'They believe materialism, greed, and selfishness increasingly dominate American life, crowding out a more meaningful set of values centred on family, responsibility and community.' This leads people to yearn for 'a greater balance in their lives – not to repudiate material gain, but to bring it more into proportion with the non-material rewards of life.' Indeed 67 per cent said they wanted more balance in their life and 62 per cent said they would like to simplify. Twenty-eight percent of those surveyed had actually taken action to downshift in the last five years.

Another point to emerge is that 'Americans are alarmed about their future'. They think that the keeping up with the Joneses mentality is 'increasingly unhealthy' and particularly damaging their children. Indeed 73 per cent of those surveyed disliked the values their children are growing up with. The Americans surveyed were also concerned about the environment and felt that consumerism and materialism were creating tangible problems. Indeed 93 per cent thought that current lifestyles were producing 'too much waste' and 67 per cent understood that America was one of the worst global offenders.

This research was undertaken seventeen years ago and so attitudes may have changed. However, given that materialism has intensified during that period, Americans may have become even more critical. And what of the influence of the 2008 recession? Tim Kasser's research shows that people's materialist values often harden with scarcity or threat and so, as he told the audience in Glasgow at the Centre's event, 'the recession is not necessarily an ally.'

But he may be wrong. In 2009 a firm of 'consumer anthropologists' conducted quantitative research in the USA with a small, representative sample of citizens. It shows that 78 per cent of their respondents thought that the American dream, as expressed through the pursuit of material possessions, had 'died' and now needed to be pursued through 'freedom and ideals'. Over 80 per cent were spending less, often through necessity but also choice. They were also saving more, getting rid of stuff and shifting priorities to spend more time with friends and family. Much of the shift in attitudes revolved round a growing aversion to debt and a desire to live within their means. This is indeed reflected in the country's falling personal debt figures. An important value in the USA is self-reliance and so the economic crisis, and spiralling national and personal debt, has encouraged its citizens to turn their back on credit and this inevitably means less spending. The UK's debt figure, by contrast, has risen not fallen since 2008.

As the US economy has for decades been particularly reliant on consumer spending a sustained fall in consumption is likely to undermine politicians' attempts to get the country back to business as usual. While this will be painful it will ultimately mean confronting, rather than avoiding, some of the big issues of our time.

Making changes

In 2003 Clive Hamilton conducted a survey for the British Market Research Bureau which found that a quarter of the British adults surveyed, aged 30-59, said yes to the following question: 'In the last ten years have you voluntarily made a long-term change in your lifestyle, other than planned retirement, which has resulted in you earning less money? This 25 per cent excluded those who stopped work to have a baby or set up their own business. Those who had downshifted were not just well-off middle class professionals but were spread across the social classes.

The downsizing often involved moving to a job which earned less money, dropping hours, changing careers, giving up work altogether or returning to study. Just over 30 per cent said they made the change to spend more time with their family, and 20 per cent did so to 'gain more control and personal fulfillment'. Almost half missed the money yet 90 per cent said they were happy with the change.

This trend has been confirmed by other studies in the UK and research in the USA and Australia. As Clive Hamilton points out, 'The emergence of a large class of downshifters in Britain challenges the main political parties to question their most fundamental assumptions about what makes for a better society.' Indeed these downshifters have made these changes despite the pressures within the system: they did so without any encouragement from politicians or the mainstream media.

People in the UK express similar anxieties to Americans about the values which are shaping their children's lives. A national poll in 2010 found that 77 per cent of people agreed that advertising to the under-12s should be banned. Again people have formed this view even though they've received no encouragement in this respect from politicians or the mainstream media.

I'm not aware of studies specifically focusing on Scotland but there's no reason to believe that Scots are bucking these types of trends. Indeed in *The New Road* (2012), the third book in this *Postcards from Scotland* series, Alf and Ewan

Young describe a number of inspiring community projects in Scotland and most involve people who have not only consciously downshifted but need no convincing of the pertinence of the issues we've been addressing.

Our capacity for change

A common conception of human beings is that we are disconnected individuals who are primarily interested in ourselves and impervious to change. But this is false. There's now irrefutable evidence that human beings are primarily social beings who cannot exist in isolation. In fact, loneliness kills people and having a strong network of friends protects our health. People are highly influenced by the views, moods and activities of others in their family or social circle. We may think that individuals are responsible for their own emotions but emotions are highly infectious.

The great lesson to be learned from all this is simple: if a single individual changes his or her life and starts talking about it to others within a very limited time this can grow from a small ripple to a significant wave of change. This is how fashions happen, new ideas suddenly start appearing in different places and we get seismic shifts in the national mood.

What next?

This is not an isolated book. It's part of a series and other volumes help flesh out some of the arguments advanced here and, more importantly, give examples of change. Nonetheless it's useful to close by outlining 11 things people can do to help put materialism, the media and markets in their proper place. More detailed suggestions are available on the supporting website[1]

---

[1] Please go to the Great Takeover section on www.postcardsfromscotland.co.uk.

1. Limit your own, and particularly your children's, exposure to commercial media – adverts, TV, magazines and websites linked into celebrity culture.

2. Take action to strengthen the various factors in your life which help promote well-being and buffer you from materialist values – e.g. relationships, family time, hobbies and interests, learning for its own sake, volunteering, physical exercise, contact with nature, meditation, and spirituality. This may, or may not, involve cutting back on work and income and involve 'downshifting'.

3. Review your spending habits. For example: Could you make a better distinction between 'needs' and 'wants'? Could you stop using shopping as a social experience and do something else instead ? Could you initiate an 'amnesty' on Christmas presents?

4. Engage other people in discussions on the themes found in this book. Remember that conversations can have a transformative effect on people's lives.

5. Try to shift your focus from individual or family wealth and well-being to community assets and well-being.

6. Take part in community or environmental activities, or start your own project.

7. Pay heed to politics and what's happening politically. Try to influence politicians' views whenever you can. Remember the importance of inequality and fairness.

8. If you're a parent, review how you see your role – are you too indulgent and focused on buying them things? Do you establish healthy limits and boundaries?

9. Take these ideas into organisations – your work, trade union, church, political party, charity, parents' organis- ations, book group . . .

10. Keep learning about the topic. Follow up on references in the text and some of the main books referred to. Visit the website supporting this book.

11. Remember you are not alone and seek out like-minded people for support.

Finally, it's easy to feel daunted by the change required so it's worth remembering that the whole system can only keep going if we buy into a set of toxic values: if we stop doing this then change is inevitable. As the anthropologist Margaret Mead remarked: 'Never doubt that a small group of thoughtful, committed citizens can change the world. It is the only thing that ever has.' □